Birthmark

Birthmark

STEPHEN CLINGMAN

November 2016

for Robert + Victoria —

with good wishes —

Stephen Clingman

University of Massachusetts Press

AMHERST AND BOSTON

First published in 2015 by Jacana Media (Pty) Ltd

ISBN 978-1-62534-228-7 (paper); 227-0 (hardcover)

Set in Sabon
Printed and bound by Maple Press, Inc.

Library of Congress Cataloging-in-Publication Data

Names: Clingman, Stephen, author.
Title: Birthmark / Stephen Clingman.
Description: Amherst : University of Massachusetts Press, 2016. | Originally
published: Sunnyside, Auckland Park, South Africa : Jacana, 2015.
Identifiers: LCCN 2016019943| ISBN 9781625342287 (pbk. : alk. paper) |
ISBN 9781625342270 (hardcover : alk. paper)
Subjects: LCSH: Clingman, Stephen. | Scholars—South Africa—Biography. |
College teachers—Massachusetts—Amherst—Biography. | Birthmarks.
Classification: LCC LA2388.S62 C55 2016 | DDC 378.1/2092 [B] —dc23
LC record available at https://lccn.loc.gov/2016019943

British Library Cataloguing in Publication Data
A catalog record for this book is available from the British Library.

To all those I have remembered
and those I have forgotten

Contents

The barrier is the gateway to the path.
– An old (and new) saying

*'Voglia': from the Italian: desire, will,
longing, lust, birthmark.*

Birthmark

1

Somewhere out there in the deeps is a planet just like ours.

They have heard of us, over there. Their planet is blue, like ours. In other ways, however, it differs. It lives in peace. Somehow there they have solved the riddle of minds, and all is in balance. They have discovered the right ratios to keep numbers stable; wisdom is replenished with youth, youth guided by wisdom. People have an integrated view of past, present and future, and live in the flow of time. Their planet is clean, and they keep it that way. Every individual has a way of embodying his or her own being while encouraging others to be themselves. They have rid self-awareness of personal adjectives; because each person is free, all combine to create the freedom of everyone. They know that contact is like a language which can be spoken exquisitely, and they learn its grammar in school. They have no empires and no promised lands. What makes a land holy in their view is what you make of it; because nothing is holy, everything is. That is why their planet is so blue, such a deep and beautiful shade of blue, much more beautiful than ours, though ours too is beautiful. It draws you in from a distance, like the most wonderful refreshing blue water. You just want to go there and stay.

I was born in the holy year of 1954. It was holy not because I was born but because every year is holy, or should be. Which is to say, it should not be more important than any other year in any other place on the planet. The Queen had been crowned the year before in

England. The Second World War was nine years over. We were six years into apartheid. My mother, who had nearly died giving birth to my brother Paul, tried it again with me. He was four years older than I. We were born into sunshine, red soil, and the short bristling grass of late summer heading into autumn. That and beautiful skies, with the Southern Cross overhead; it made you want to run outside in the garden all night with everything sparkling and wheeling above, the dark air like a current warm and cold.

Not too much money for us there, then. Our first home was in Kempton Park, which was where my mother's parents lived. Where had they come from? Like my father's, from the other side of the world, an unknown world on the other side. Lithuania, Latvia— Riga, Kovno, Krosz: these were places that echoed only as a distant and receding language. But we were not from there. Our place was so insistent, so lucid, so clearly the present that the past was like a dream one forgets in the day. Only my grandparents knew that dream, now a place of irrevocable loss. Although our parents knew more of it than we did, to us it was essentially unknowable, an invisible point of origin from which time, in which we lived, had emerged. It still ebbed and flowed in the undercurrents of our sensibility, muted sounds in certain rooms in the darkness, but we were drawn outdoors to the brilliant sun, the grass and warmth and the dazzling, incommensurable light.

The old question: where are you from? Unanswerable, except in segments, various parts of the truth which, even if it were known, could not be fully told. Well, first we came from Africa, because all people did, and we migrated north. Somewhere along the way we got lost, then found. Then we moved again, and again, until we ended up in Kovno. There were pogroms, and suffering, and bad weather, snow and mud. Then we returned to Africa again. And then we left. It is not so different from anyone else's story, if you think about it.

Memory does not come continuously like a stream, but only in layers and fragments. Meaning is made out of space, and the spaces between.

✑ 2

He was born into light, the most beautiful soft and bright sunlight of the most beautiful place on earth. At least, that is how it is in my memory, this other self who was me, the presence within me still. When I was born, we lived in Kempton Park, near my grandparents. My mother's father Isaac had come to South Africa when he was thirteen; his father was a rabbi, a pious and learned man, and a scholar whose every gesture encoded gentleness. His name was Rabbi Moses Friedman (affectionately known as Reb Moishel or, in the pronunciation of the day, Reb Meishel), and he had been a founder member of the Beth Din in Johannesburg, then a town still in turbulent transition after its beginnings as a mining encampment. Though bookish, Reb Meishel had certain saintly qualities. Before he died, he begged forgiveness of anyone he might have harmed even unknowingly; when couples came to him to be married, he would always ask the bride, 'How old do you say you are?' so as not to embarrass her or cause her to lie. This sort of delicacy of the unspoken became an underlying motif for the family, so that the slightest undulation in tone could have major significance. We were trained readers of those shifts from the start, sometimes a burden as well as a gift.

When Reb Meishel died, there were thousands at his funeral, the papers reported, and a train of cars and carriages more than a mile long. The rabbi delivering the oration mourned the loss of a *Talmid Chochom* who had 'lived in his books and died among them', studying the holy Torah in the quiet of the night while others slept and a world of wars and strikes went on about him. Meishel's son Isaac, however, was different. A bit of a dandy at heart, an entrepreneur, he became mayor of Kempton Park, a small town to the north-east of Johannesburg. In an act of biblical repetition, Isaac married Rebecca, the daughter of a man who came to Zuurfontein before its name changed to Kempton Park; he had walked from Cape Town, where his ship had docked, across the expanses of the Karoo and beyond into the interior. He was named Max Kahan, and he began his life in South Africa by selling groceries to the British soldiers from a siding at the railway station in Kempton Park after the Boer War. For all these migrants there were chronological gaps and asynchronies. Parents preceded children, children preceded parents, husbands preceded wives in the vast journey across the oceans until those who remained behind could be brought over to join them.

Isaac, the son of the rabbi, joined Max, the father of Rebecca, and they ran a grocery shop in Kempton Park called Kahan & Friedman, where my father also worked many years later when it had become a hardware store. After Max's death, his wife Esther moved in with her daughter and son-in-law, and so my mother grew up with her widowed grandmother in the house, a woman who hauled herself round on crutches and mourned not only the children she had lost but also the impure country she had come to, the *trayfe land*, where the proper ways had fallen behind. She herself was so godfearing that all the way on the boat from the Baltic via England to South Africa she had lived on a barrel of salt herring, knowing nothing else could be guaranteed as kosher. One can only imagine what state she was in when she arrived—and perhaps what it was like to be near her. Sometimes it was the other grandmother who came to the house, Reb Meishel's wife Rosa—she would sleep with one eye open in the bedroom she shared with my mother. For Esther, now suffering from short-term memory loss, there was nothing like the country she had left behind, but when my mother asked her own mother about that forgotten place, all Rebecca said was why would you want to know about the mud and the snow, the shacks with indoor kitchen fires that could burn the house down in winter. It was all best left behind, and though there were memories of those who remained, in that time goodbye meant goodbye forever.

Still, the house filled with the sounds of Yiddish at times, a murmur in the background in the night when parents did not want children to understand. Or men would arrive for the Jewish holidays, soup dripping down their beards as they ate, and ever after my mother had a horror of beards. When my grandmother tried to speak Afrikaans to some men who came to the door, eventually one asked her politely, 'Ag, mevrou Friedman, praat asseblief Engels, laat ons ook verstaan'—'please speak English so we can also understand'. Rebecca's view was that if the Afrikaners didn't much like the Jews, at least they were open about it; it was the English who would smile at you while fondling the knife behind the back.

These are the stories I was told, stories that became true for having been told; they are as true as I heard and remember them, though no doubt I have some of it wrong. Heard, misheard, remembered, misremembered, no one knows anything more than three generations back. At least not in our world, the world we came from, because half of that world disappeared, and now it is disappearing again.

It was the world I was born into, under the Caesarean knife in the Florence Nightingale Nursing Home in Johannesburg, from which I was taken back to live in Kempton Park. Naturally I remember nothing of this, not least because when I was two we moved to Johannesburg, some twenty or thirty miles away. It was quite a distance in those days. So then the memories do come. There was the house, the bright and sparkling newly built house, with its rounded embankment along the road. For that, trucks had come and dumped soil, there is a vision of them tipping up, way up, high up into the sky, as the sand and rocks came tumbling out. Then my father made a picket fence, painted white, to line the border of the property, but the termites came and ate it, and it had to be taken down. From the road go down the driveway, the beautiful pastel slasto driveway to the dark heavy wooden front door with its knocker, the bronze head tinged with green of a woman from the sea and the electric doorbell, into the coolness of the entrance hall inside. The house itself is stippled white (with a slight pink tinge), low-slung and long, elegant and modern with its red-brown tiled roof from which we jumped onto the grass when we were older. Underneath the flooring were the foundations, which you could get to through a trapdoor in the passage and explore crouched over with a torch in the dark. On the other side of the house, the world opened up. Here was the lawn mowed to within an inch of its life by my father every Sunday, where my brother and I and our friends would play and run, with another embankment leading down towards the lower lawn and the high brick wall at the end topped with shards of tinted broken glass to stop people jumping over. There were canopied jacaranda trees whose purple flowers appeared in early summer and whose latticed leaves gave the most delicious shade. There were the hedges, one in the garden, one lining its edge on the eastern side, where you could find hollows and natural hiding places; and at the end of the garden grew bamboo, which you could cut down for tree houses or huts.

This was the world that became my world, and when I was born, so my mother said, I was bright and lively, with a ready smile and laugh. There is an early picture of my brother and me, the younger one standing on a chair, the older sitting next to him, looking up with love. Later that wasn't always the case, or at least temperament sometimes led to explosions, but why not, that is how brothers are. But everything was there for the making and taking. One day, in the new house, when I was already at school, my grandfather arrived, my father's father, a stern and distant figure who frightened me more than a little. Through the kitchen window I saw him park his car at the top of the driveway, and emerge with a dog which he leashed and walked down to the front door. No one home except myself and Johanna. My grandfather rang the bell, came into the kitchen, and asked for some old blankets for the dog to lie down; then he turned to go, making his way up the driveway. Fraught with anxiety, I ran after him. 'Sir,' I called, 'you forgot your dog!' But the dog was for us. He was a spirited black-and-white fox terrier named Laddie, a character and a roamer who lived with us for many years.

So there was the smile and laugh (so I am told), an intrinsically joyful spirit. Around six months, then, a new appearance, just there under the right eye. It was the black line of a birthmark edging the lower lid and lashes like dappled facepaint or luscious eyeshadow. And it lined the upper lid as well. What to do? Anxious parents consulted, doctors in the family recommended doctors. One doctor said wait, leave it alone until he is seventeen and has finished growing. But the other, a plastic surgeon with a penchant for tricks with a knife said it's dangerous, it must come off right away, and I am the man to do it.

Birthmarks: the markings of birth. Everyone has them, but this one was to be taken away, so it would live on only in its absence like all those half-remembered worlds.

3

What I see: I see green. The dominant impression is green.

This was what happened. When that new presence in my life first appeared, the furry lining under my eye, nothing in my vision or enjoyment of existence was affected in the slightest. I still laughed the same way, played with the same spirit, smiled the way I always had, saw without any problems at all. For convenience, everyone called it a birthmark: euphemism, yet also identity. Yet, naturally, my parents were concerned. They turned to the first line of approach, the doctors in the family, the brothers-in-law. One said, leave it alone for a while, he's small, things may change. The other, a gynaecologist, said it must go, though how his specialty qualified him in this regard wasn't clear; perhaps he was just used to the invasion of bodies. Referrals led to the eminent Dr P, who had made his name in the war conducting reconstructive and cosmetic surgery for airmen who had been burned or disfigured. This was honourable work to be sure, though later Dr P became an almost mythic adversary for me, a haunting figure of fate. I was taken to see him (image in my mind of his rooms), and to him the work must have seemed both natural and inviting. There were medical concerns: later on the growth could become cancerous. But equally significant were questions of appearance. Think of the complications and the cruelties of others, the dimmed prospects for happiness, because it looked like nothing so much as a black eye. Still, the decision was not easy for my parents; there was much soul-searching before, eventually, they went ahead when I was two. I would have an operation to remove my birthmark.

So off I went to hospital in Hillbrow, near the nursing home where I was born, for a second birth of sorts, to emerge this time more immaculate, pure. Out of the womb of home, I entered a land of hard surface and steel. And then into the place itself, with its lights and covered faces over me. They put something over my nose and mouth and called it a balloon. They asked me to blow it up, and I tried with all my might, proud as always of my willingness, my capacities. What I remember then is green—the green of the operating theatre, or maybe the surgeon's and nurses' clothes, or perhaps it was the green of the ward where they kept me afterwards, or the green door I was not allowed to go through. Some forty years later, when I am doing my vision exercises, looking into the mirrors of the stereoscope and trying to see with both eyes, this is the moment when the pain comes and the burning and the tears, and something deeper than I know. But am I remembering or imagining? Is the feeling the memory, or is it a memory of a certain feeling? And do I then lend images to the horror and the terror? Consciously or unconsciously I look up as the surgeon approaches. I see the knife, the sharp steel coming towards and seemingly into my eye. I cannot shout, I cannot scream, I cannot turn away. Left eye turns inwards, horrified but also transfixed by what it sees. Right eye does anything to veer away, to look away from what is coming, turning outwards towards something, anything in the distance. The scream is inside. And then it is all gone. I am gone.

After the operation, they kept me in the hospital for ten days, because there were dressings and all kinds of things to take care of. The doctor had removed skin from my arm or thigh and used it as a flap to cover the area he had excised, standard cosmetic procedure. I was not allowed to be in contact with my parents, in case I cried and ruined the surgery, so they saw me through a one-directional glass.

12

They could not hold me. In the ward on my own I was a little hero, made to feel special. Nurses fussed, there was ice cream and a large bunny with big teeth, and eventually a glorious homecoming. The great Dr P's work was done, and he was no doubt satisfied, but over the next while a curious thing happened, for the birthmark began to grow back. It clearly wanted to be there. It was not quite the same, however—not the same beautiful black with clear outlines and undamaged lids. Now the lower lid under my right eye was bumpy, raised in parts, tear ducts damaged, with eyelashes turned inwards in the near corner, to cause me trouble forever. The flap was half there, half not, a strange kind of layering, grafting, chimera. So I had to confront the world like that after all, except not exactly as I had been before, unadulterated. What had been my eye was now also a wound.

In later years there was discussion. Did I want a second operation to have the birthmark removed? The wisdom was that I should wait until the age of seventeen or eighteen to decide. My parents found a way of being straightforward about it. For a long time we agreed to call the birthmark my 'black mark'—a fact I completely suppressed until my mother mentioned the word again decades later. By the time I was seventeen or eighteen, however, I wanted no more of surgeons and their ways. This was who I was, black mark and all. I was ready to take my chances. But underneath, things had begun to change, and what we see on the surface is not everything that occurs. Underneath, left eye had continued to focus inwards, right eye to veer away from contact and encounter, something I now had many reasons to avoid. Left eye was beginning to see close, right eye continued to look out in the distance. And if the eyes were doing that, so was the mind. It became a way of seeing, a different form of awareness, a split form of existence. I would never see quite the same way again.

Here and there, there and here. Left and right, dark and light, double vision. The divided consciousness inherent in our lives in that place became accentuated in a personal way. It was nothing major in the history of the world. It did not compare with what others were suffering all around me in my own country because of the markings of their skin. But in this one body, in this one mind, things had begun to shift, at first imperceptibly, later more noticeably. My new lifetime had begun, my second birth with and without my birthmark, a strange dynamic of presence and absence, of being there and not.

4

I am in the neighbourhood: right into Mons Road and then right
again, and then down a bit and left a few blocks to where my friend
lives in a flat on the second or third floor. This is unlike our house
with the garden and all the space in the world to play. Here we are
on the balcony, looking down into the street. Down there are the
only adults who walk in Johannesburg, black men making their way
from one place to another. My friend makes a face, goads, says listen
to this, and shouts something down. He goads again, taunts, says
you do it too. Reluctant at first, I get into the spirit and shout, shout
something down at the black men. One of them looks up. When I
go home, I tell Johanna what I had shouted. Telling her must mean I
think there is no problem about it at all, that this is the most natural
thing in the world. Perhaps it means that in my eyes she is not like
the black men; after all, she works for us. But if there is pride in my
voice, perhaps it is there only to hide my uncertainty. And for once
Johanna is angry. Her anger is as cold as it is hot, and she rebukes
me with the clearest intensity. People are people, she says to me, they
are human beings no matter what, and don't you ever forget that.
As soon as she speaks I know she is right and I am deeply wrong.
It is the first mark of my shame, and I never do it again. It is enough
shame to last me a lifetime.

Johanna was in our household for as long as I can remember.
She lived in a room off what we called the yard—a courtyard really,
though of a very functional kind, floored with concrete. The yard

separated our part of the house from the servants' quarters, where Johanna and the others—the gardener Stevens (his first name) and his predecessors and successors—lived and ate and perhaps loved in a series of small rooms where their beds would be raised on bricks. The laundry was on that side of the yard, and in the middle was the double-T of the clothesline stretched along most of its length. The back door, painted red and made of iron, led out to the embankment and the road, and locked with a clang when you slid the bar. Every now and again I might visit Johanna in her room, the air dusky and smoky, not a space where I would have wanted to live. But in and out of that room, and in our rooms and our house, Johanna worked for us, cooked for us, collected the laundry, talked with me. There were few things I liked better than being with her in the kitchen while she stirred the ingredients for chocolate steamed pudding and let me lick the residue from the mixing bowl. No accident that I was with Johanna when my grandfather brought us Laddie, our dog. She was my second mother, and at some level I loved her.

She always felt enormous to me, immense, and she was quite fat and waddled a bit, though the one remaining photo I have of her shows her surprisingly young and really quite small. But Johanna had a big personality, and could be fierce as well as generous. Here we were at the intersection of her Xhosa and our Jewish culture, and there would be crossflows of one kind or another. When I was small she guided me in the ways of 'number one' and 'number two'. I remember her exclaiming '*Tshini Thixo!*' with its extraordinary click, a phrase I translated roughly as 'Good Lord!' or 'Good God!' The first time I heard the word 'rape' was when she and my mother were discussing someone in the neighbourhood who had been raped, though neither of them explained it to me, and in our world you never asked. Johanna knew things about me that no one else knew.

The yard was our common space, and on certain summer nights when the joy of living was almost too much for me I whizzed around it on my beloved Raleigh bike—just the right size with its straight handlebars and Sturmey-Archer gears, round and round and round, up to a hundred circuits anticlockwise (everyone has a favourite direction), cutting the corners on the small quadrangle, brushing the clothesline poles at each end, left knee raking close to the ground as I banked. I would go out there after supper, under the stars, because the yard was open to the sky, and exercise my body and spirit in sheer exuberant joy. Who knows what Johanna and the others thought of it as they went back and forward to their rooms dodging the little human missile, but they tolerated me. Eventually, I would peel off, happy and exhausted, ready to drop into bed and the next day's pleasures.

In the yard, especially in later years, Johanna would host her women's church group, and they would sing, filling the space with profound and full-throated harmonies. On Christmas Eve, old man Halamandres from around the block would take our Johanna and their Johanna (as I recall, they had the same names) to midnight mass at the Cathedral in town for one of those rare moments when the racial filters of apartheid fell away and all worshipped together. It meant not a bit to Mr Halamandres, father of my friend Johnny, that he was Greek Orthodox and this was a Roman Catholic ca-thedral. For all I know, he may not have gone inside himself, but it was his clear act of piety and generosity once a year to transport two black women to church, wait for them and bring them home. I tried to imagine it, but couldn't really; between the Catholicism, a service in the middle of the night, and the people all worshipping together, the very word 'mass' made me feel rather queasy. I also couldn't imagine my father ever staying up past midnight to take Johanna or anyone else to church—something he would never have done. But those harmonies in the yard rising into the heady summer night, that was something never to forget.

Why did I take Johanna so much for granted? Why does she

come into my dreams now, as she has taken to doing? Where did my cruelty come from? Some of it might be explained away, but not by me. I was young, absorbing the ethos of the world I lived in, though my parents would have been horrified, for they taught us lessons of fundamental respect. But a friend goaded and encouraged, assured in his sense of the normal. I took the bait and shouted things from a balcony down into the road at people walking by. I may have been young, but I haven't forgotten, and nor has Johanna. Nor have her children and her children's children.

Present and past, here and there. As much as I regretted that moment, I regret the neglect in later years. We met some of Johanna's family, her son Raymond who came to visit her every now and again. He was separated from her for so much of her life and his. At times I would reflect on it, what it meant, and how strange it was: the life he had to live, the one that was open to me for no other reason than a difference in skin colour. How had fate played its tricks, what would my life be like if I were him? And there he was, in our yard, a little older than me. We were mirror images, he black, me white, looking at one another and contemplating the divided paths of our destinies. I think Raymond struggled at school; I did not. He needed things. My parents would give.

But the truth is, I turned away. I did not keep in touch with Johanna, whose warmth had once enveloped me. And why was that? I know that by the time I left home I felt removed from my existence, like someone trying to walk on a floor that tilted away beneath me at a distance I could barely see, floating above it without any foothold or grip. The servants saw and watched us; they knew more about us than we ever did about them, our most intimate details. But it was not so much this that disturbed me. It was a system in which I felt trapped, divorced from myself, and having servants in the house was an intractable part of it. Later, in Johannesburg, we would be faced with a choice ourselves: someone desperate for a room, please

18

I will work for you, please don't turn me away—and we didn't turn her away, Edith and her small daughter Abigail. Johanna too needed the work, and my parents helped her family. At least they stayed connected.

But I did not. Deep down I was shamed by the realities of such a life and could not get beyond it, of having people do things for me that I wanted to do for myself. I wanted to feel reality, touch it and taste it, to know what it was like, and reality felt nothing like the life we were living. I turned away from Johanna out of shame, my shame, and it is my shame that I turned away. I did not pay attention, I did not stay true. So, Johanna is in my dreams, and she has questions for me to answer although she died many years ago.

5

We are taking you down to see the Devil.

I am at my cousin's house, the big one in Parktown, where my aunt lives with her husband, the famous gynaecologist. Boys all over Johannesburg are given his first name by grateful mothers, so there is a generation of Joels in the suburbs. Things are not so happy in that house, however, for Joel's interest in female anatomy has taken an unsanctioned turn, but that is another story, told ultimately on the back pages of the *Sunday Times* where in the 1960s a divorce featuring a gynaecologist and an heiress is big news. As for me, I am the youngest on this side of the family, my mother's, a place I hold with some sense of pride, though sometimes being so young and excluded can be excruciating. This is an authoritarian society where seniority counts for everything, and to be the youngest is to be the squib, the tadpole, the squirming creature of no consequence whatsoever. My brother is closer in age to the cousins, but the cousins are distant figures and live in another world.

I would see them at Passover at my grandparents' in Kempton Park, a magical time. We would arrive early, and my small grandmother would be at the oven in the kitchen making *kneidlach* for the Seder, the matzah-ball dumplings that tasted so good, especially at the beginning of the holiday week. Ritual tasting followed—familial rather than religious: tell me, how are these, have a taste, I made extra specially for you (if she said this, she said it to everyone). The men would go off to synagogue—the word embarrassed me, what a strange word, but *shul* was also quite odd; wasn't there some language in which this would be cleaner, different, its own? At a certain point as I grew older I joined them. And then back to the house for the Seder, all around the table with the blue crockery imported specially for Pesach, the silver cutlery. They read the Haggadah, those older men, my grandfather and uncle Harry especially, and when it came to the songs they would race through them in absolutely tuneless but hilarious old-man versions, so that spirits were always high. When the food came, there was egg in salt water, the soup with the *kneidlach*, the matzah, the horseradish (give me more *chrein*, my father would say), the main course. My job was to sing the four questions—why is this night different from other nights?—and I did it year after year because I was always the youngest. I learned it with pride, sang it with pride, knew those questions by heart, accepted the compliments afterwards with flushed happiness (there were some perks to being young after all). But I also watched my older cousins, who knew so much, did so much. They played marbles with the Passover nuts, which of course would never run straight, giggled with one another. They tasted the four cups of wine, and either through real inebriation or its simulation would end up lying under the vast table. Later, when it was all over, we drove home from Kempton Park with the full moon following in the window, for the holiday was linked to the moon—a sleepy and peaceful experience which ended only as the sound of the engine changed tone and the car began its turn down the driveway.

Elsewhere, I would see the cousins from time to time, though not that often because there was a difference between my parents and theirs. Joel and Harry were doctors, while David's father Julius was a lawyer; mine worked in the hardware store in Kempton Park until he struck out for better prospects. One day at David's house, while his mother Cissie was still alive, I was sitting on the grass in my shorts when suddenly I leapt up in agony, attacked by a whole hive of red ants. There I remember cool interiors, criss-cross *riempie* furniture, leather lawyerly volumes. At Erica and Mark's I would marvel at the tomboy Erica who walked on stilts and could go higher on a swing than anyone I knew. Erica had suffered polio as a child, and was quarantined at the Children's Hospital, a place of dread for us, close in proximity as well as imagination to the nearby prison, the Fort, dug into the hillside up the way on Hospital Hill. Erica's was such a serious case that, in my mother's words, it had 'burned itself out', leaving one of her arms thinner than the other and affecting her prospects as a dancer. Now she was a tomboy because, as she put it later, it was the only way to be with the boys all the time. Mark was genial, the oldest and therefore the most distant. One night there was a party at their house, and Mark indulged me by playing records and allowing me to guess the titles, which, following a rule of tracking the most repeated phrase, I usually could. Mark also told a joke which for some reason I never forgot. Which Chinese author wrote 'Mark on the Wall'? The question was confusing because my cousin's name was Mark. The answer was Hu Flung Dung; I laughed, but didn't understand it.

Now in the big Parktown house it is different and much more dangerous. The day has begun with the cousins—not all of them, but it would be saying too much to reveal who—telling me they can walk through walls. They disappear and reappear, and though I don't believe them, there is part of me that does, and I cannot work out how they do it. My brother is part of it too, though perhaps less willingly, I don't know. And then it comes. All right, come with us, we are taking you down to see the Devil. How can they do this to me? Why do I go along? They take me to the broom cupboard under the stairs, and close the door. It is pitch dark in there, yet even so they tell me to close my eyes, because it won't work unless I do. I close my eyes and hang on tight. They press buttons, make the sounds of a lift going down, down, down, down into the depths of

22

the earth. All the sounds of chaos surround me, and then we reach the end. OK, now open your eyes, and I do, and all around me I see devilish faces lit up and leering at me through the dark, making wild noises. The broom cupboard is suddenly vast space and there I am—and I scream, at which point they tell me to close my eyes, they will save me, they are taking me up again. Sounds of the lift going up, and the door opens to let in the precious light of day, and I take in sheer gulps of breath. The voices then are consoling. Are you all right? You won't tell anyone, will you? See how we protected you and brought you up to safety.

There are many mysteries about this event. Not only why they do it, and what compulsion or satisfaction they feel. But even more profoundly, why I let them do it to me, more than once. Why am I so docile, so accepting? Is this my way of belonging, of being with the older children? Is it simply that I cannot resist their blandishments and authority? Is it partly out of perverted generosity, allowing them to do what they apparently need to for their lives to have meaning? Whatever the reason, this seems to be my role, but inside it is a lesson I come to understand. Those who claim to save you are the ones who have come to torment you. It is a principle true of private life as it is of the political universe, and in it are written the intricacies of families and of empires. Later I will never go into small closed dark spaces.

6

In early summer his father would take him out onto the front lawn, down the slasto verandah steps, the grass just beginning to unbristle with its new green shoots, and there would begin a ritual that lasted all season long, and over many years. The boy was all padded up, by which I mean he was wearing his cricket pads strapped onto his legs, padded batting gloves on his hands, maybe (depending on his age) a 'box'—otherwise known as a protector—inside his underpants, and a beautiful cricket bat in his hands, all sanded and oiled for the glories to come. This was first of all where my father taught me the care of things. When, because I was growing, there was a new bat—oh the joy of it!—first we took it into the bathroom to 'steam', that is to draw in steam from the bath, sweat a bit, release its inner spring and bounce. Then lovingly we sanded it and applied linseed oil in three coats, with its distinctive and unforgettable smell. Finally, the bat would emerge, the product of patience and anticipation, an underlying ethic for a lifetime. And God forbid you should let it just lie around or drop carelessly to the ground. It wasn't retribution that would follow, but something far worse, a sound in the voice, something that would happen to him, not me, severe disappointment.

Out on the grass, my father overturns the white bench and places it just in line where a ball struck towards the overgrown hedge lining the garden will be caught in its horizontal slats. I take my place in front of the other hedge, which sometimes in winter serves as a

goal for soccer; my father is ten to fifteen yards away. There I take
up my stance, patting my bat to the ground, head turned to face
my father, who doesn't bowl overarm to me in the usual way, but
instead throws the ball with an overhead motion, placing it here and
there with steady deliberation for me to practise my shots. How do
I learn? From the very beginning my father is methodical, teaching
everything like a grammar. We explore the foundations in categories:
forward shots on the front leg, back-foot shots stepping back, from
simple blocking shots to measured drives (always on the ground)
which send the ball on the off-side to my father's left and on the
on-side into the ball-catching slats of the bench. Forward defensive
shots and attacking; backward defensive shots and attacking,
until the reflexes barely need asking for a decision. Always form is
crucial, and here the lessons are clear: timing and poise will do what
aggression will not. A well-timed ball elegantly stroked will speed its
way to the boundary just as quickly as a spectacular wind-up will
produce, if not more so. Beauty is an inalienable part of the process.
And then we proceed to further refinements, more elaborate phrases
in this fundamental syntax. The nuance of the backward cut to the
boundary placed with perfection will get you four runs using the
pace the ball already has from the bowler. And the crowning glory:
not a lofted shot as you might expect, for in this school the ball is
never lofted, but the delicate, almost nonchalant leg-glance, where
the ball is glided and re-angled with the lightest of touches beyond
the reach of the wicket-keeper down to the boundary. And if there is
a fielder in range, you will get at least one run or perhaps two, not
bad when you want to keep things moving along or need to get the
strike at the other end.

And beyond that: how to map in the mind where the fielders are,
so your shots will go between them, or short of them, or beyond
them: think in negative space for placement. My father puts spin on
the ball, shines it to induce swerve, though this is hard to reproduce

25

in the garden, throws harder and faster, some balls pitched up, others short so that a backward 'pull' is in order, all instant-fast, all with the eye on the ball, all with perfect form, for form and function are one. The boy learns to fear nothing, there is an inner serenity, a calm alertness, a readiness to pounce on any opportunity. At the age of nine I go with the school team to see my first major cricket match, at the Wanderers, scarcely able to breathe with the excitement, unable to believe that those people out there, on the field, are the famous MCC, the players I have only read about, they are real—look, there is Ken Barrington! At ten I am playing for the school first team. At eleven I am selected for the Transvaal provincial team, facing up in the practice nets where the selection process is completed to boys of thirteen almost twice my size who bowl with unbelievable speed and bounce. Though my reflexes are on maximum alert, under a clear hot blue sky I am unafraid of it all, I measure myself up to the speed, dispatching the ball confidently in all directions. At twelve I am captain of the school first team, but when the provincial selections come round again, I am only vice-captain of the Transvaal; I am quietly told the captaincy must go to an Afrikaner, the politics of the day demand it.

Later it all goes corrupt, all goes wrong, but this is the glorious season when I can picture myself, with some certainty, one day donning that green cap with the gold springbok on the front, playing for South Africa, facing up to bowlers as fast as Peter Pollock and taming them with the fabulous timing of his brother Graeme. But when a friend asks which cricketer I would like to be, I give an honest answer: I don't want to be anyone else, I just want to be myself. I would go with my father now to other matches at the Wanderers, and there we saw the last Australian team to come for some decades. They too had green caps, wonderful caps, dimpled on the sides at the peak. We would park miles away (my father's planning: no traffic when we leave), carrying a hamper with sandwiches and drinks that my mother had prepared. There in the stands, my father beside me, I would study tactics, so that when I was captaining my team, my coach would say to me, you have a *yiddishe kop*—a Jewish head—with the finer points all pinned down. Because of that he would let me run things on the field, slowing the game down when we were in danger of losing, altering the field placements to prevent or sometimes entice runs, deciding on the change of bowlers, everything.

Some of this would never go away—the belief in timing, elegance, seeing the whole pattern on the field in considering a de-cision. Strangely, my father was not that way himself, for he had a temper and could be impetuous. When he played cricket, he would loft the ball for the fences with a studied attack I never attempted, let alone achieved. But the affinity for the underlying grammar of things remained. That was how my father taught me to drive a car as well as play cricket, and in the next generation it was how I taught my daughters too, oblique continuities of philosophy and style. Later my father, who never read a book, would be up at four in the morning doing cryptic crossword puzzles, and people would phone him from all over Johannesburg to get the solutions.

⁓ 7

On the way between Johannesburg and Kempton Park is Gillooly's Farm, and if we are travelling in the daytime, sometimes we stop off there. We park the car and find the cool shade, and maybe we have a picnic, and there is grass greener than anywhere I know, because there is a stream. It is rural and countrified, unlike the veld, and unlike the grass at home which is short and springy in summer, short and brittle in winter. This is different, however; is this what England looks like? The road continues towards my grandparents, and some-where along the way one day, as we approach the townships my grandfather has established (these are for whites to live in, not the black townships that lie on the edge of my consciousness), there, in a field, is a herd of cows. The boy—me, I—is transfixed for reasons he can't quite understand but which slowly rise within him. They seem so slow and peaceful, those cows, so much in and part of the landscape. He looks at them for a time that seems out of time in the car moving by, and then makes an announcement. When I grow up, I know what I want to be. What is it, they ask, what would you like to be? When I grow up, he answers, I would like to be a cow.

There is mirth—one of the cousins is in the car—but also some curiosity. A cow, they ask—why? Because they are so slow and peaceful, because they aren't trying to do anything, they just are, they're just *there*, moving their jaws from side to side, eating grass in a field. This, almost literally, is his ruminative aspect, wanting peace and thought and serenity, a kind of eternal contemplation. Since then he has always had a special feeling for cows, though his aunt Sheila will come to say she can't abide them because of the resources they use up. In his own life later on he moos to them whenever he sees them, deep and sonorous with a semi-serious face, and they come up to talk. Once, in England, we saw a herd of golden cows with their calves head down to a beach as the sun was setting and wade serenely into the water.

That is one part of him, but of course there are others. There is soccer, and early on the fierce little creature who could say this to Mrs Johnstone from next door: 'You cluster duster! I'll smash you and I'll bash you and I'll crash you, and when I'm done I'll fold you up and break you into a million little pieces!'

What had occasioned the eruption? Mrs Johnstone next door was a swimming teacher. Her house had a pool, quite large, and a small one next to it known as the baby pool, where she began her lessons with the children, stalking up and down in her starched short-sleeved white cotton dress that came down below the knees, her large-brimmed straw hat on top, and blowing her shrill whistle, a rather fierce personage. I was fascinated by what went on there, and would climb over the low breeze-block wall to look more closely, trampling Mrs Johnstone's flowers in their beds. She would ask me to get out and go home, but one day, when it must have been too much, she lifted me up bodily and placed me back over the wall, warning me in very clear terms not to do it again. That was when my outburst occurred, to live on in family lore. But Mrs Johnstone and I got on famously as well, because I too had begun my lessons there. First lying on the hot slasto tiles next to the baby pool with my face immersed in a plastic bowl, getting used to the water and turning my head to the side, learning to breathe like a swimmer. Then floating face down in the baby pool, arms outstretched. Then to the big pool, starting on breadths and then lengths, where at an early age I could swim, and became a demonstration model for others.

Who is that little boy there, with such different sides? As time goes on he will get used to being quite symmetrical in some respects, asymmetrical in others, both inside and outside. There is left, there is right, there is up and down, here and there. Swimming gives him bodily harmony, and he will practise on his bed, lying face down and turning his arms and kicking his legs as if doing the crawl. It flows into his soccer, his cricket and everything else, an immersion he is quite used to in body and mind, the organising polarities of his being. As for that bed, I remember it well, especially with the green cover it had later, the dark-brown tapering posts at head and foot.

We lie down at night, six inches or a foot off the ground, horizontal in a room, just like those cows coming back to the same field. We wake up in the morning in the same room, and think we are in the same place. But during the night the room has moved; the earth has revolved on its axis and shifted in its orbit round the sun. The sun with its planets has been spiralling around the galaxy, the galaxy in its cluster also moving, the whole operation expanding and moving at some unknown velocity. Who knows how many directions we are moving in at once? And yet we wake up in the same bed and think we know where we are.

Is the self who was then the one who remembers now? There have been many rooms and beds since then, many spirallings, turnings and returnings to a place that is not the same. Yet that bed with the green cover is still there, the cows are in the field, they are on the beach, the boy is still saying cluster duster, the combination of disparate elements still the name of his game, the dialectic between stillness and movement still the inner rhythm of his being, interpretation the form of his life, not least in looking back to the cows, the bed, and the swimming pool over the wall. Still in that car from Johannesburg to Kempton Park talking to those who might want to listen over here. Still talking to myself, looking, thinking, moving still in this landscape.

30

8

It must be my brother's eleventh birthday, and I must be seven, only just. All my brother's friends are there on a beautiful early May afternoon just beginning to crisp in the autumn; I may even be wearing my favourite blue-and-black striped flannel shirt with grey shorts, which I got for my own birthday. At a certain point the activities turn to soccer, unorganised around the garden. Here I learn that I have a gift, because I can dribble around my brother's friends, holding them off, getting past them, putting the ball through their legs. There is a feeling of joy and illumination running through me, and some of my brother's friends compliment me afterwards, something I am not used to from older boys.

One day, with the soccer season now approaching, I came home and told my parents that I was going to the trials for the under-ten team at school, and I was going to get in. I had made up my mind, and had no doubt I would succeed. My parents must have been indulgent, willing to let me try, perhaps not believing anything would come of it, wondering how to prepare me for disappointment. But to me it was a settled question; there was simply no doubt at all. So I went to the trials, with probably nothing more than a pair of 'tackies'—flat-soled tennis shoes—on my feet. When I returned, that day or the next, I announced to my parents that I had been selected. I was in the under-ten 'A' team, and would play inside-left. For me the fact may have been expected, but the feeling was nonetheless extraordinary, and the only thing that could match it was when my mother took me up to Squires in Yeoville to buy my soccer jersey. It came in a cellophane wrap, and had large red-and-white squares and long sleeves, with a collar and lace-up V-neck. I can still remember the smell of it as I put it on for the first time in the garden at home, feeling little short of bliss. The socks too were gorgeous, bright red with white foldover tops and a white band halfway up. The only problem was my boots. Like much else, they were hand-me-downs, coming way above the ankle, and instead of studs they had cork bars running crosswise on the soles. They worked after a fashion going forward, but if I tried to turn it was like slithering on ice, and I would end up ignominiously on my backside. So there was compromise. Though my parents couldn't afford much, they bought me some solid—that is to say, inflexible—ankle-high boots with moulded rubber studs, and I could play.

I played in the under-ten team for three years. In one game, when we were two-nil down, I remember thinking that I simply had to take charge, and so I did, scoring a hat-trick to win the match. For the last goal I ran the ball all the way up the field on my own, not my usual method but it had to be done, and at the following practice the coach made everyone stand in a circle around me and bow down, which made me feel embarrassed. At home I practised all the time. I would put a line of stones spaced out along the grass, and dribble between them. Then I would tighten the space and do it again, right foot and left foot. I practised dribbling with two feet, forcing myself not to look down, until I knew where the ball was, as if it were tied to a string between my feet. That was how to bedazzle the opposition, because you could see which way they were leaning, feint and do the opposite, while they had no idea what you were going to do. Using two feet you could squeeze through the tightest of spaces. Decades later I saw an interview with the incomparable Pele, who relayed the advice his own father had given him as a child: you must learn to play with both feet. For myself I believed that profoundly, and my aim was to use each foot with complete parity, whether for dribbling or shooting. I took some pride in calling myself ambipederous; who knows where I got the word from.

One winter I went to camp during the school break with my brother. Such camps were unaccustomed in South Africa, but the man who ran it had seen summer camps in America, and this was his way of testing out the possibilities. My brother and I went with my mother to get bedding roll-ups and ground sheets—we couldn't afford sleeping bags, or they were too pretentious—and we slept in the cold tents at night after songs around the campfire ('A froggy went a-courting and he did ride'). The mornings were fearful for me, especially the breakfast line—will I have to drink cold milk?—but in the midst of it all a god appeared, the great, the very great Sir Stanley Matthews from England, whose jinking runs along the right wing I had read about with nothing less than awe. Who knew what had brought him here, but there we were one afternoon on the small soccer field with banked sides, which I loved for its self-contained and compact feel, and here was Stanley Matthews coaching us and watching us play. This could only happen in heaven.

Now the ball has gone out of play, and it falls to me to throw it back in, but all my teammates are marked. That's all right, for I have it worked out in my mind: I will throw it to one of my players and get the return pass as I come onto the field. But suddenly Sir Stanley stops the game as he sees me look for a player to throw to. 'Wait,' he says, and asks me, 'who is the only unmarked player on the field?' I look around, and I look at him, and 'There isn't one,' I say. 'Come on,' says Sir Stanley, 'who is the only unmarked player on the field?' Again, regretfully, I have to tell him there isn't one, because especially by now everyone is marked. Again, with increasing exasperation he asks the question, and once again I have to say there is no one, until finally, he says to me, 'Come on, boy, it's you! *You* are the only unmarked player on the field!' I know what he means:

he wants me to throw the ball to one of my players and get the return pass—exactly what I had intended. But his phrasing had been wrong, and that was the confusion. 'But sir,' I say, 'I'm not *on* the field.' It's true: throwing in, I have to be behind the line. My love of soccer has competed with my feel for language, and I pay the price. Sir Stanley thinks I am taking the mickey, but for me there is only a sense of injustice mixed in with my adoration. Why didn't he ask me, why didn't he give me a chance to explain? I already *knew* what he wanted me to do. Why couldn't he understand?

When I was ten, another breeze blew in from paradise, the storybook kind, except it was true. I had already played my under-ten game against the visiting school, and thought of going home, but for some reason stayed around to watch the school second team play, and then the first. These were the big boys, the twelve- and thirteen-year-olds. But the second team was in trouble; some of the boys were sick or had not arrived, and they had already used their reserve player and needed one more to make up the full side. The coach found me there, and asked whether I would like to play, because they could use me on the left wing. It wasn't my position, but I barely needed asking. I played and scored, lofting the ball from the sideline over the head of the goalie when I saw him off his line, an inspired and accurate shot. After that the coach told me to come to practice for the first and second team; I played for the second team a few times, and then suddenly I was in the first team. Some of the older boys resented it—always the accusation: you are too big for your boots, almost a literal complaint in this case, though in reverse, because it was more like the boots being too big for me. Now I saved up my money—all of eight rands—to buy low-cut Puma boots, the best kind, and the same as the most dashing first-team players wore. Very little could compare with the feeling of low-cut Puma boots fitting snugly below the ankle. I polished and cared for those boots with devotion.

34

One day, playing in my inside-left position, a teammate sent a rolling pass towards me some twenty yards out and started off on a run, wanting the pass to be returned. But the subconscious that was pure body had taken over. As if in slow motion, I saw the ball rolling towards me at just the right pace, and over there I saw the goal and the goalie, and the inviting space opening up on his left. The ball moved towards me, I moved towards the ball, and instead of returning the pass, I struck it so beautifully, timed it so sweetly that it began to make its curving way towards the goal, and the goalie could only watch as the ball sailed by him, curving and rising upwards into the top corner of the net, which it hit with the most satisfying, inimitable rippling sound.

One is humble after such moments: we are taught not to celebrate or exult, and along with my teammates I turn to go back for the kick-off. The boy who had wanted the return pass has an air of grievance about him, as if I have done something against the rules of decorum in scoring such an outrageous goal. But it is unassailable, perfect. There the ball is, still rising and curving forever in my mind, just about to rip and ripple into the back of the net. That is what I want to do, that is who I am, that inside-left soccer player.

9

He is lying in bed, and his father is stroking his head. It feels nice and comforting, but it is also not nice, because his father has been away again on one of his absences. His father is a remarkable person, with tremendous will-power, and also a temper. One night at the dinner table, after he had left the hardware store in Kempton Park where you could make no money, and started his new job at the department store in Johannesburg, he announced that he would double his salary within a year, and did so. He took opportunities, going to Cape Town for a while as regional manager for the company, and that was when his career took off. The boy's mother went to join him in Cape Town, and sent postcards back with pictures of seagulls; she loved being at the sea. While they were gone, he and his brother went to stay with family friends. One morning their friends' father walked into the large room where they were all sleeping and asked cheerily who could tell him the name of the President of the United States. Quick as anything, because he was quite proud of such things, the boy answered 'John F. Kennedy'. 'No, it's not,' said the father. 'Yes it is!' said the boy, insistent be-cause he knew the answer, and knew that he knew it. 'No, it's not,' said the father. 'John F. Kennedy's been shot, and it's Lyndon B. Johnson.'

He and his father have a special relationship. In the early mornings he goes into the bathroom where his father is having his bath and spends what seems like hours there talking and relaying his thoughts, whatever is on his mind, all his ideas. He may peek into the bath, to see that large bushy root floating there, so unlike his own. He knows these mornings are special to his father too, who mostly just lets him talk, on and on and on. On weekends he and his brother go with his father to the school old boys' club (a strangely accurate phrase), where his father plays hockey in winter and sometimes still a bit of cricket in summer. As time goes on, the hockey team his father plays for is called the Old Crocks, which takes him a while to work out. His father has his rituals, stopping off on the way to buy mini-packets of Chiclets gum for the match. During the game, he and his brother gravitate towards one of the goals and talk to the goalie there; one of their favoured players is called 'Bles' and has a moustache like his father's. After the match the men go off to the showers, which the boys sometimes go into, a place of mystery and steam. Then his father and the others are off to the bar while the boys play outside, and sometimes have to go in to call their father when it is getting late. Romantically, he pictures himself as a waif having to call on his dissolute father in a bar. The club, and especially the bar, are not Jewish, a fact he absorbs through a kind of osmosis from his mother. Yet some years before, his father has been selected to play hockey for Maccabi, the national South African Jewish team.

On Sundays his mother stays home, because everyone will be coming for lunch. The two great-aunts arrive, and his grandmother, all of them stone deaf. 'Bessie,' says Great-Aunt Sheila in her Yiddish accent, which all of them have, 'would you pass the salad?' 'What?' says Bessie, the ash lengthening along her cigarette. 'I said,' repeats Great-Aunt Sheila, 'would you pass the salad?' 'What?' says Granny Bessie. Great Aunt-Sheila repeats herself one more time, to which Granny Bessie responds, 'I can't hear you. Would you like some salad?' Also there at lunchtime is Auntie Essie, who never married but takes special care of his cousin Denis and his family;

Denis's father Baruch is a political prisoner. In later years Essie's driving—for she is the one who brings them all—becomes erratic, and once she goes through a stop sign straight into a brand-new Porsche which the owner had bought the day before. 'What a lovely accident,' Great-Aunt Sheila announced gleefully when they arrived. 'No one was hurt.' Or rather, in her accent, 'No *vun vas hurt*.' These lunches drive his father crazy, and he retreats to his big brown chair in the lounge as soon as he can, but his mother has no such refuge.

Sometimes in summer, though, his father is the cook when they have a *braaivleis* outside. When a storm comes up and there is a danger of the fire going out, his father stands over the barbecue with an umbrella. There is a photograph of him leaning over it in the darkening sky, lightning flashing all around. His two grandfathers come, Isaac from a game of bowls, and Louis, who had brought the dog. Louis does a somersault along the ground, something utterly unprecedented and never repeated, though it is mightily impressive. There must have been something in him after all.

So it is quite nice to have one's head stroked late at night in bed when you have already been asleep for a while, but not so nice, because some days or weeks earlier his father had left along with his bags. At home, at times, there is temper and anger on all sides, both his father and his mother; things go flying, and his father will regularly offer to cut his throat if that is how they all feel about it. Once, when they are driving with his mother, they see his father in a car with a woman. These departures happen with some regularity, and the way they are usually resolved is when his father will arrive home at night, and father and mother will retreat behind the closed door of the bedroom where a huddled conference ensues with muted voices emerging. One Sunday night when his father returned to the front door and rang the bell, the boy wanted to hit him, and his anger was boiling over as he confronted his brother in the passage. Later it got even worse for a while.

38

His mother did not want her children to be deprived of a father, and feared the consequences in a time when divorce was a scandal, especially in light of what happened to her sister, whose husband's professional and personal interest in female anatomy was matched only by his interest in money. Yet during one of these absences his mother announced with some finality that this was it, and she would live on her own with the children. 'I have strong shoulders,' she said, and meant it. She took the boys on a drive towards Rustenburg, but they never got there, for the younger one saw the Magaliesberg mountains looming larger as they got closer and began to cry uncontrollably, convinced that the mountains would fall on them. His father returned some time later, as usual.

You might deduce from this that the trauma was endless, that forgiveness never came. There was trauma no doubt, but there was also loyalty and longing along with the sense of betrayal. As for forgiveness, that is a very complex word, but something hard to name arrived when his father died many years later in the most extraordinary way, and it brought its own kind of unclenching, something like peace. What, in all this, was real? The early morning talks in the bathroom, the headstroking, the absences, the women in cars, the anger, the returns? All of it was, in this strange and entropic world in which we agree to live.

⌐ 10

In the photograph, my grandfather Isaac is on a horse in Kempton Park, bandolier over his shoulder, looking quite cavalier, to use the appropriate term. The year is 1922, and he has been summoned in a state of emergency, for the white miners have come out on strike, an event that will ultimately involve an aeroplane bombing their holdout in Johannesburg and a few executions. It is a moment full of contradictions, for this is when the miners, marching under a Communist Party banner, exhort the workers of the world to 'Fight and Unite for a White South Africa'. My grandfather appears to be against the workers, but perhaps he had little choice when called out by the government, and Kempton Park, where he is making his respectable way in the world, is in any case far from the centre of the action. There were other ripples, other oddities in the moment. For Smuts, the prime minister and redoubtable anti-imperial guer-rilla fighter during the Boer War, had long since aligned himself with British imperial and mining interests, while my grandfather— the *shtetl* boy grown up to different things—had much sympathy for Afrikaners who had suffered under British imperialism, and once stood for office as a Nationalist.

On the other side of my future family were relatives who would have supported the strike. One, Great-Uncle Charlie, was involved in politics in Russia, and like many others had to be sped out of the country for his safety, helping to found the new Communist Party of South Africa. One of Charlie's nephews—my father's cousin

Baruch—found his own way through a radical Zionist movement to Trotskyism, and in 1964 began a nine-year sentence in the Pretoria Local and Pretoria Central prisons for sabotage as a member of the African Resistance Movement. Thus do the family currents mingle and diverge. One lineage is rabbinic and mayoral, while the other wants to make the world new for and by revolution. We are somewhat nondescript in the middle, or perhaps we have a little of each.

How do these stories go? The man on the horse is the son of a rabbi, but it is on his wife Rebecca's side that the string of rabbis really goes back and back, according to legend for some thirteen generations until they meet up in a glancing way with the Vilna Gaon, the holy, wise genius of Vilna. Of course everyone claims to be related to the Vilna Gaon, though genealogies will later give some weight to our credentials. But here, in this new country, much of that history is lost. And there are other losses. Rebecca loses her sister Sheila, and brings her nephew Cecil into the house to live as one of her children. Others die, and it is hard to keep track of the accounts: some in the flu epidemic, one (after whom I am named) in unrequited love (hushed rumour had it) in England. One went to Palestine to be buried in Jerusalem on the Mount of Olives. Later, those who remained in Lithuania died in the very worst circumstances, until there was no one left that anyone knew of.

My father's family had their own stories. They too were immigrants, from the Latvian–Lithuanian border. Their name originally was Oswinsky, deriving perhaps from a Lake Oswin in the area, but in South Africa it changed. On arriving in Cape Town my great-grandfather Naftali decided to go into a venture with another new immigrant named Klingman, and to make things easier adopted his name. Later, when the First World War broke out, his sons Charlie and Louis changed the initial letter to a C, so that it would appear less German. Louis was my grandfather—the strange and taciturn man who left us the dog—and he had a reserved relationship with my father, never showing any overt interest in his life. But once, when my father's knee was broken in a rugby game, my grandfather carried him bodily to the doctor. And once he came to watch my father playing cricket, sitting distantly in the stands and never saying a word about it. His wife Bessie was pretty but flighty, and she became a virtuoso at baking and at cards. Every Sunday she would bring around a chocolate cake for us, prepared according to our varying preferences, and she taught me how to play rummy. She would sit—and play cards, and bake—with a cigarette dangling in her mouth, ash lengthening along its end until it seemingly defied the laws of gravity, while we all looked on enthralled. We suspected that sometimes it was the secret ingredient in her cakes.

There was tragedy in this family too, however, for the eldest, a daughter named Rita, had died, to leave a lasting hollow, an echo which no one, including my father, spoke about. Later my father's cousin Lionel wrote to me about her. Rita was perhaps four years older than he was, Lionel told me, full of zest, bright, active and cheerful. Yet somehow she came down with typhoid fever, and was taken to the fever hospital; she was very ill. Eventually the doctors were satisfied she was beginning to regain her health, and her parents were enormously relieved.

It was late May, Lionel wrote, and a public holiday was coming up. Louis and Bessie visited Rita in the fever hospital, and explained that her aunt would come the next day while the family went on a picnic. The following morning, as they were preparing to leave, there was a ring at the front door. A policeman stood there with the news that Rita had died during the night. There were shock waves throughout the family, and Lionel vividly recalled his aunt Lily in the passage of her house talking over the telephone while her children stood and watched, utterly absorbed as she wept, the tears pouring down her cheeks.

42

'The next morning,' wrote Lionel, 'all the children were brought together in our house in 23 Hendon Street while the adults went to the funeral. There was a pall of sadness over us all. Some time later Louis and Bessie and Reggie and Stanley came to live with us, and how we all found room to fit in, I do not understand. Auntie Bessie remained bereft, and every Sunday morning without fail she and Louis would visit Rita's grave. One Sunday morning we children were playing a board game on the floor when Louis and Bessie returned, and Bessie threw herself onto a bed, weeping inconsolably while Louis tried to comfort her. My mother appeared and quietly ushered us out of the room, closing the door. Eventually their family moved into an apartment in the new Olympia Mansions in Yeo Street, opposite Lily. For a long time Bessie kept a large framed photograph of a cheerful, confident Rita on her bedroom dressing-table.'

That was Lionel's account, and I myself recall seeing the photograph of Rita on my grandmother's dressing-table, though I did not know who she was—just a dark and mysterious presence from another time that one could not, would not, ask about. And so it was that my father grew up in a family of three sons, to mirror almost directly the four daughters in my mother's. For him, the sister he had loved was gone; I imagine it was an absence in his life and outlook ever more. At the age of eight he was now the eldest, and he could not make it up to her or to his parents. I think she was the sister in him, a female presence marked by her loss, a softness hiding somewhere which few would ever see, which perhaps even he would seldom acknowledge. She had gone, a mark of his birth taken away, living on as a memory always fading into the distance.

↶ 11

We were told that our Grandpa Isaac's father, Reb Meishel, went with his son at some stage to Germany. He had developed a pain in his throat, and eating was difficult. The doctors in South Africa diagnosed cancer, so the community raised funds for him to see a specialist overseas. They duly arrived and saw the specialist, who told my great-grandfather he would operate the next morning. That night, however, the doctor died, and the following day Reb Meishel saw a younger doctor who looked in his throat and discovered a fish-bone lodged there. The doctor extracted the bone, and father and son returned to South Africa where Reb Meishel continued to live and work for many years. So it is that some surgeries are best avoided.

One night in our house in Mons Road, I woke in the small hours to hear unaccustomed sounds coming from my parents' bedroom. My room was next to theirs, and earlier I thought I had heard something—a phone ring, steps down the passage, the front door opening and closing. I must have gone back to sleep, though later I might have heard my parents return. But this sound was different. My parents were in their room, and there was a wailing coming from my mother such as I had never heard before. I thought I also heard consoling sounds from my father, but it was the wailing from deep down that I remember. When I got up in the morning I learned that my Granny Ree had died. She had gone into hospital for a cataract operation, and a thrombosis had developed. She had been ill, relatives had visited (she had told one of them, if *you* have come to see me, then I must really be sick). We had been kept secret from that, cushioned, protected as always. And then this. My Granny Ree—Rivka, Rebecca—the tiniest, biggest-hearted person, who gave each of us half-a-crown when we became taller than she was (I was sure I would never get mine, but she lived long enough for me to get it too)—she was gone. Rivka had a lively word for everyone, an alert tongue that got to the quick, for she had a flashing intelligence which all her hard years of work in the house had not dampened. One she would call a *luftmensch*—he had his head in the clouds; beware if you were just a *vilde khaye*—a wild animal. She seemed to sum everyone up. The grandmother and her daughters were a maternal band that ran everything in our universe, even if the men did their best to wrest control away.

There were other departures. Cissie was the first of my mother's sisters to go. She had wanted another child, and was given hormones and medications that made her ill and depressed. Later it seemed that the doctors had killed her. When she was nearing the end and my mother was visiting her in hospital, she heard one nurse say to another too loudly that this one was not long for the world. Cissie was unconscious, said my mother, but she turned her face to the wall. David, her son, came with us that year to my beloved Oyster Box Hotel in Umhlanga Rocks, a quiet presence in the car and on the beach. Isaac himself died when he was living in our house, blind now, and after a few strokes had left him more or less incapable. My brother dressed him, his driver William drove him. He got into a fight with my father who was driving us one day, because the road was too bumpy. Once my brother accidentally hit his car, a new Chevy, with his cricket bat sticking out of its bag as the car was coming out of the garage. It had a dent, and what a tin can the car must be, we thought, in defence of the cricket bat.

When Grandpa Isaac was ailing, my parents sent me off to

stay with a friend. There I showed off, pushing my stomach out at dinner with my shirt pulled up, as if I were pregnant. The parents, rather austere colonial types, were silently aghast, and the father later had his revenge when he operated on me to take my tonsils out—for he was a highly respected surgeon. When Isaac died, as in the case of Rivka I could not go to the cemetery because I was too young. Everything happened off-stage for me. That night, there were memorial prayers at our house, but it was 5 November, Guy Fawkes, with fireworks everywhere except for us. I could not go to the prayers, so I went outside in the night to see the rockets exploding distantly over the sky, feeling sorry for myself and slightly ashamed of my theatrics even as I did so. When Grandpa Louis died of a heart attack, my father met me at the gates of my school and took me home. By then I was sort of getting used to it.

In about 1961, there was a departure of a different kind, one that initiated a whole new era for us, a kind that previously would have seemed unimaginable. My aunt Sheila and her husband Harry were leaving for America with their family. This was prompted partly by political crisis—the Sharpeville massacre and the State of Emergency which followed—as well as a general revulsion for apartheid. But also Harry, who was a medical researcher, had been offered a job in Virginia where he would have better opportunities for his work. And so they left. Sheila had been a member of the Black Sash, the women's anti-apartheid movement, and was involved in resisting Christian National Education; one can only guess what leaving meant to her by what happened afterwards. We went to see them off at the airport, from all sides of my mother's family. Normally, the airport was a special treat. You could see the huge aeroplanes that looked so small in the sky (I would ask my brother: how do they fit the people in there, Paul?) and wave to the passengers from the balconies. Inside the building was the statue of Alcock and Brown, the first men to fly non-stop across the Atlantic. But this time was different. The small boy, observing, sees his Granny Ree begin to weep as the goodbyes are said. He goes up to her and asks her what's wrong. Granny Ree says, I will never see Sheila again. Yes you will, Granny, of course you will, he says, surely you will see her again. He looks at her consolingly with his eyes and hugs her as the tears come.

Sheila had known loss before. During the war her dashing young man had gone off as one of the first South African pilots to join the Royal Air Force in the Battle of Britain, and there was shot down and killed. It was afterwards that she and Harry were married. Sheila was a beauty, and so was her pilot; Harry was not like that, and he could be as gruff as anything, but he had an abiding loyalty and love. Now, at the airport, the moment of her own departure from home, Sheila took it all in, saw her mother, saw her weep, saw the boy hug her, saw the look on his face and his grandmother's, and never forgot it. My grandmother, however, was right. Not only did she never see her daughter again, but Sheila could not even come back for the funeral from America.

There were other agonies, for in Virginia she found a world more backward in its racial views and politics than anything she had known. Whereas she felt at home in the landscapes of South Africa—profoundly for her the very origin of humankind—and a purpose in her political organisations, there was little for her in Virginia. She became ill, and would sit on the side of her bed for hours, smoking a cigarette while it ran down. There, without reading or watching the news, she knew what was happening in the world. The doctor came and said, you're in a depression, and Sheila smiled because she knew it was literally true as the mattress sank beneath her, hollowed out where she sat. She was sent for shock therapy. I can only imagine what it must have meant to her to be violated and convulsed in that way.

Many years later, I came to see her again, and she told me some of these stories. She made me understand how she had always felt a bond with me, because of the way I had looked at the airport and spoken with her mother. Though she said she would never have advised me to come to America, in her later life she moved with Harry to northern California, and was happy there, for its grasslands and hills and flowers reminded her of home. She had her own wisdoms by then, a special feel for the stars, for ecology, the connections between all things, life and afterlife in the transformations of matter into energy and back. As for me, I tried to glean all I could from her, in her oblique pronouncements, her time-capsule clues, her understanding of how the universe worked. She always gave the feeling of knowing much more than she could say. For her, words were inadequate, to be used only sparingly and allusively. So she would drop whatever seeds she was able to in her way, for me to pick up as best as I could.

12

I am ten years old and everything is perfect. The body is perfectly in balance, and in harmony with the mind. This is pre-puberty time, when the whole self, such as it is, has reached its fullest, most integrated expression just before the disruptions enter in; nothing will ever be like it again. What the mind wishes to do, the body can achieve; what the body prompts, the mind conceives in the same instant. The eyes still feel perfect, left and right working deftly together as two hands, forward and back a continuous pathway in the world. We play in the garden, I ride my bike in the yard and in the streets, a skateboard appears which I will use to career down the hazardous slopes of Bezuidenhout Street. It seems a capacity for audacity has always been there; if I imagine danger it is only to take it on as a kind of dare. When I was quite small at the Oyster Box Hotel, I ventured out onto the massive granite rocks on the beach, fascinated and attracted by the suck and spray of the waves, until an enormous breaker came and crashed all over me. I held on for dear life, and Johanna, watching, was horrified, but I returned like a buccaneer triumphant, glistening, mouth open, with water.

There at the Oyster Box I remember the beautiful aquamarine pool in front of the hotel above the beach, and the smell of the red rubber inner-tubes in which I first floated, discovering the idea of swimming as bright water lapped all around. There was a luminosity in that pool, a sparkling presence it is hard to describe, such a beautiful shade of summer blue. Everything stood out as if

49

in an extra dimension, like the cola tonics at the hotel, or the ice cream which came in little pewter bowls with wafers standing alert at an angle, brought by the Indian waiters dressed in white. We tried to befriend those waiters, learn their names, but they, polite, maintained a dignified anti-magnetic field, so we would not get too close. Down on the beach we flew aeroplanes tethered by strings like kites, the wind whipping the wings around on their horizontal struts, keeping the planes aloft. Only David, who helped us with the planes, was subdued, because his mother had died.

Now at ten, the luminescence is intense, to be discovered and rediscovered every day. I explore every cranny in the garden. In the corner at the bottom we cut down the bamboo, curving and latticing it with leaves to make huts to sleep in, though when night comes we are always a little too terrified and never make it through. Down there at the bottom the wall is topped with broken glass to prevent intruders coming in, but in the corner I can loft myself up to go to my friend Tim's house, across on the diagonal and leaping over the roofs of the servants' quarters, then down on the other side. At Tim's the cricket coach sometimes arrives; in later years he went blind, and used others' eyes to make his decisions on team selections. Sometimes he phones me at home to talk about things and chide me when I say 'Ja' instead of 'Yes'. What is in it for this teacher, and why is he calling me at home? I don't know, and though it is a little flattering, it also makes me feel a little strange.

In the garden everything happened. That was where the birthday parties took place, and my brother's became wild. We formed up in teams, ranging over the neighbourhood, finding and capturing one another. One of his friends set up a trap down the passage alongside the house, and a boy nearly broke his leg running through it. My cousin came once and knocked my brother unconscious on the verandah, demonstrating his karate chops, at least ostensibly. Once my brother knocked himself out on the Slip'n Slide, which we went slithering down in the garden. I too suffered injuries when my brother used me as a demonstration model to show his friends how cowboys in the movies only pretended to knock one another out, except that he forgot to stop short before clattering my skull with his metal toy pistol. Or he and his friends would hurl clods of earth at one another, and one of them didn't see the stone in the clump he was throwing, catching me in the head once again. One needed a special kind of fortune to survive such a childhood unmangled.

But on other days, on my own, a kind of bliss descended. I knew every leaf in the hedges, the garden was my domain, and I left it too, so that Eden extended beyond the gates—perhaps because there was no gate to this garden, it just ran up the embankment onto the street. It is into the street that I go, walking, walking in the neighbourhood and beyond, left down Mons Road towards Innes Road where I turn right down the steep incline and then up the other side towards my Hebrew teacher's house, but I don't go there, oh no, there is no way I am going there. Instead, I head up the hill towards the observatory from which our suburb draws its name. But the observatory is closed, and that isn't my destination either. Rather, I turn left along Observatory Avenue opposite the house where my brother and his friend David once blew up a pile of gunpowder, singeing their eyebrows and swearing me to secrecy.

From there past the nursery school on The Curve from which I had nearly been banished. That happened because the teachers made us drink cold milk, which I hated, and also gave us squishy, overripe bananas to eat. Once it was just all too much, so I squooshed up my banana and threw it at one of the teachers. Of course I was not one to miss; my father said it was a photo-finish as to whether they could withdraw me from the school before I was expelled. After that I went to Clara Patley, the school adjoining the Yeoville Synagogue. There I played the triangle and the drums: what a revelation to feel the roll of the sticks in one's fingers in time on the skin of the drum!

And how the body can actually climb up and over that rope jungle gym! There sometimes I would sneak out, playing hooky to go and visit my uncle and aunt, Michael and Ethel, who lived in a flat on the corner. And there too, in the playground, some of the boys would chase the girls to pull up their dresses and pull down their panties. It made me uneasy, and once I stood up to them, though it couldn't have been enough, because I remember a lecture to us all from the school principal.

Now, down and past The Curve, the landscape stretches out towards Cyrildene where my friend Alan used to live. The *koppies* rise to the south, and I am on an outcrop of the ridge too, glittering all around in the sun. I turn left, back towards the golf course, and then left again into the street of perfection. Here everything seems magical, from the quietness of the road to the soft purple of the jacaranda buds and the spangled shadow cast by their leaves, the feel of the sun on my skin, the scents in the air of spring or summer. If lawns are being watered there is the hiss of their sounds, wafting wet grass or earth. My body feels new and strong and lithe, modular and light, my mind a zone of serene and transcendent contemplation. Here aesthetics, mind, body, spirit come together and I have a sense of understanding which I cannot explain but simply feel where I am in the dappled afternoon light. I tell myself in a conscious moment of decision that one day I will return from wherever I am to live in that street. I can still picture it today.

13 ⤳

Two and ten seem to be the markers, and everything happens in-between for the boy, the he that was I, the I that was he. He and his brother are companions of a sort, but only to the extent permitted in a world where a gap of four years creates vast differences in rank and authority. Paul is a maker of all things—model railways and aeroplanes—and once tries to construct an actual aeroplane out of old doors and assorted paraphernalia. Paul is also fast on his feet, incredibly fast, and the younger one imitates him as he practises his starting technique in the garden for races at school. The two become a single-bodied double-headed monster, the younger one turned upside down and holding his brother's ankles while his brother holds his elevated feet. They walk around the garden like that, a lumbering two-headed Frankenstein's monster. Paul also flies model aeroplanes, the kind that have real engines and fuel, going round and round in a circle controlled on a length of double-line and a hand mechanism. Most of them are designed after US or British planes from the Second World War, but once Paul gets a German Stuka which can dive and release bombs—an odd choice in retrospect.

The younger one is officially the assistant in these ventures, though occasionally he is allowed to take charge. Once, when he tries to fly a plane and crashes it, a dark mood descends on his brother, and there is the threat of physical danger. In that regard the younger one has to be highly attuned to subtle shifts of feeling in tone, when a rising temperature in the atmosphere will suddenly distil into anger. He is a kind of property to his brother, at least it feels that way, but if they are out at the sports club with their father, it is Paul who defends him when other boys comment on his black eye or attack him. Paul is the only one who is allowed to attack him, that is clear, but he is grateful for the defence, almost sentimental about it. Paul is the one who has the name: it is clear and concise and dashing, like him. The younger one wants a name like that, and for a story written at school invents a figure called Robert Trent, the name he would like to be.

At school he goes into Anderson House, like his father and brother before him, a tradition. One day, in Grade Two or there-abouts, the teacher asks him to take a message to one of the high-school boarding houses, across the cricket fields and behind the looming shadows of the oaks. He goes, full of trepidation on an anxious journey, up the dark path to the house, not sure if this is the right house or whether he should be at some other, or what will happen to him when he knocks on the door. But someone takes his message quite placidly, and he returns trembling. In Grade One they take a spelling test after learning some of the basics and everyone misspells the article *a* as *u*, except for one boy who gets it right be-cause he had failed the year before and remembered it. The teacher has a fierce reputation, and makes boys who misbehave stand in the large rubbish bin outside the classroom. The night before the first school assembly of the year he is terrified, because he doesn't know whether he must go to his classroom first thing in the morning or find his way somehow to the school hall. One day, he and his brother get each other's sandwiches by mistake. At break he takes a bite and recoils in revulsion—that awful jam!—but when he runs all over the school to find his brother and warn him before it is too late, his brother hits him for having taken a bite of his sandwich.

At school they use Stephens' Glue and later Stephens' Ink, which makes him feel special, because he is Stephen. Early on he also loves the interlocking S-clasps of his elasticised school belt not only because they click so perfectly together but because they double his initial. Later, schoolmates who are jealous of his sporting success isolate him on the playground, turning games of tag into vicious physical encounters. Discerning what is happening, he retaliates, chasing after one boy and diving on him from mid-air, bringing him crashing down to earth where the grass is worn away to hard ground. As his father never tires of telling him, it is not the size of the dog in the fight that counts, but the size of the fight in the dog. Once, when an Italian boy calls his friend Mickey, who is Afrikaans, a bloody Jew, he defends Mickey by launching himself across his desk and punching the Italian. Once he and his good friend Daryl, whose father is the *gabbai* at the synagogue, explain patiently to a teacher that the reason it is raining is that the Jews have prayed for rain during the festival of Shemini Atzeret.

At school the seasons operate according to their own logic. Marble season arrives mysteriously, when boys will set up piles of coloured marbles both before and after hours for others to shy at; the big ones are called *ghoens*, and the most exquisite have rainbow-coloured striations in the glass. During break there will be times when the boys play 'fly', setting out their ties for a kind of hop-skip-and-jump. For gym you carry your tackies in a small bag, and when he himself is small his bag is a beautiful soft-blue flannel decorated with white sheep. In athletics season his mother makes him a rosette to wear, and Anderson is yellow-gold, the best, far better than Grimmer, which is pink. This is a world which ensconces and envelops him.

And so there I am, entering that world once again. Now I am with my best friend Alan, who lives with his family in Cyrildene. Alan has the sweetest nature, and comes over to the house to play, or I will go there. At Alan's it is the shadows I remember, not so much of the house but of a feel in the air. Alan's siblings are much older, though I always have a memory of Pam, a distant figure who nonetheless radiates a special presence. There are pictures of the two of us playing soccer at our house—me with arms extended as if in a ballet, toe pointed after the ball as I kicked. Alan wasn't as good at soccer, but took genuine pride in my achievements, and I loved him for it. Suddenly, when we were nine, he disappeared, and it seemed as if he had died. It wasn't Alan who had died, however, but his mother, of ovarian cancer. These had been the shadows in the house. Later I learned that he had gone to live in Pretoria with his aunt, where she too, like her sister, died of ovarian cancer some years later. In this way Alan lost two mothers, a grief that must have been nearly unbearable. In high school he returned for a while, but by now we were in different worlds, and then he disappeared again, gone to Israel with his father, where he served as a paratrooper and began to make a new life. The Alan I once knew was sealed forever at nine in my mind.

Years later in Amherst, the phone rang one Sunday, and my daughter announced, it's Alan, for you. My neck and spine tingled; it felt like a ghost returning from the dead. Alan had tracked me down, and was living in Long Island with a wife and two sons. We spoke, and soon saw each other, and it was as if he had never gone away. He was exactly the same unutterably kind and generous person. But now it was his sister Pam who was ill with ovarian cancer, carrying the genes of the family's female line, and we were able to visit her just once. As we entered the room where she half sat, half lay on a couch, I felt the same aura, the same magnetic spirit I had sensed as a child, the same quiet presence punctuated by an undeniable spark and passion. She spoke of stem cell research, saying that one day it would save people like her. Like my aunt Sheila, Pam seemed to have an innate sense of who we are and what we are meant to do, knowing the vastness of the stars, the need of the dispossessed, the nuances of the smallest things. Some months later, she too was gone, and I could only be grateful to have seen her again, to marvel at the cycles through which our paths cross one another in various places and times, allowing us sometimes a second chance of a kind.

⌒ 14

But at home the bike was still there, and the road, and the soccer and the cricket, and the sunshine, and the joy, and the walks past the observatory into the most perfect road in the world. One day, riding my bike outside our house, I decided to make a U-turn without looking back, and a car coming up behind nearly killed me. I careered left into De la Rey Street where my friend Johnny lived, and the driver came after to give me a lecture on the preciousness of life, including my own. At Johnny's house we would turn somersaults on his trampoline and then go inside to listen to the Beatles sing 'Eight Days a Week' while allowing round chocolate pastilles to dissolve deliciously in our mouths. Every now and again boxers turned up to train in the garage, for Mr Halamandres had been a boxing manager for a while, and there may even have been a glimpse of one of the famous Toweel brothers arriving. One afternoon at Johnny's I ate some sandwiches made the way only their Johanna knew, in triangles with the crusts cut off and the softest bread. On the way home I suddenly remembered it was Passover and felt crushed, for I was not supposed to eat bread. However, when I got home and confessed, I was forgiven as always. Later Mr Halamandres, who had visited America, opened Johannesburg's first steakhouse and made his fortune.

When my grandfather Isaac came to live with us after my grandmother died, the house was extended. My parents' room became his room, and I was given a room alongside theirs. There was now a second bathroom, and the garage too was lengthened to take two cars. That meant a new extension on the verandah alongside it, and a blank wall just waiting for my parents' friend from down the street, the artist Cecil Skotnes, to come along and say he was thinking of going into murals, and could he use our wall to try out an experiment? Of course my parents agreed, and so one day Cecil arrived with a friend to begin work. Soon we had an amazing piece of artwork to live with every day, which with its swirling greys and blacks and figurative suggestions combined Cecil's African explorations with the Nordic feel of his antecedents. Cecil would come over for a drink sometimes, hair swept back elegantly over his head, a moustache like my father's, his left eye beginning to droop as the evening wore on; he had fought in Italy and told us his stories. Years after, when our house had been sold, we were told that the orthodox family who bought it had knocked pylons into the mural to provide the structure for a *sukkah*. By then they had built a huge wall around the house too, for what is orthodoxy without a hard sense of boundaries. No more Eden reaching beyond the gates of our garden.

The elongated garage meant a longer roof as well, extending just to where the jacaranda on the other side of the verandah reached over with its branches—perfectly convenient for making the leap onto its corrugated surface. That roof was where I hid out sometimes, especially on afternoons when I had Hebrew lessons to attend. I would pretend to fall asleep there, hoping no one would notice until it was too late. Unlike most boys our age who went to *cheder* at the synagogue, my brother and I had private lessons with Mrs Ludwin, who as it happened lived in the house my aunt had once occupied near the street with my favourite walk. There we read Hebrew primers with a distinctly modern feel: *Gad yeled gadol*— 'Gad is a big boy'—and the children in the pictures wore short shorts and the little blue hats of the kibbutzim of the 1960s, when all the illusions were alive. Sometimes, walking into the dark European living room of the house (so different from the images in those books), I'd find out that I was to be taught by one of Mrs Ludwin's children—the grown-up Sam, who was training to be a doctor, or one of the twins, David and Tamar. During one lesson I got into a raging argument with Sam, not over anything Hebrew or biblical, but over when 'its' should get an apostrophe. Sam was in a loop, I knew that, but was insisting over and over again that a sentence like 'The cat licks its tail' should get an apostrophe, whereas 'It's raining' shouldn't. I held on, tigerish, and it became very fraught, because in our world he was older, much older, and studying medicine, and therefore by definition knew better. David and Tamar impressed because at the age of thirteen they fasted on Yom Kippur, walking the long distance to *shul* and back, dry-mouthed and almost fainting by the time they returned.

The synagogue in its heyday was a place of irreverence as much as reverence, which made it palatable. We went mainly for the high holidays, but could afford seats only for my parents, so my brother and I would scavenge places to sit down, or hang around the *bimah* where the cantor sang, and if you were lucky you could find space on the steps. The Kol Nidrei service on the eve of Yom Kippur seemed absolutely endless that way, a completely exhausting dirge filled with a sense of ungraspable meaning. And then you would go home and stay hungry. My friend Daryl's father presided over the proceedings in his *gabbai*'s top hat (what a strange mix this was, somewhere between *Fiddler on the Roof* and *My Fair Lady*). The rabbi had a reputation for spraying, so the word was that when you stood in front of him for his sermon on your bar mitzvah, you'd be well advised to bring an umbrella. Back in the seats—where there'd be space during the course of the day as the *shul* filled and emptied in its own kind of systole and diastole—the men would exchange stories and the latest jokes, until the rabbi turned on everyone with

60

a glaring eye. When we returned in the afternoon on Yom Kippur, genial Mr Sapire would inspect our tongues to see if any food or drink had passed our lips. Smelling salts would do the rounds for those feeling faint; we'd take a sniff and recoil from the fumes. My mother, looking down on it all from the women's quarters upstairs, was quite sure that the rabbi could see my father sleep through his sermons, while for us, looking up, it was clear that men simply had more fun than women. At frequent intervals, all the young ones would pour outside to jostle, gossip and flirt. On my bar mitzvah, the Christian boys in my various sports teams filed respectfully into the synagogue, many of them wearing school uniforms.

Through all this the boy floats in the bath (he has found a way of levitating by holding his breath in a certain way) and dreams of being great. In *shul* he wishes he could offer some commentary like the rabbi does, because he feels he has much to say. Or that someone would decode those big books for him, begin to show him what they mean. He wants to be wise, he thinks he might be Jesus, maybe he will be the messiah, but no, that is presumptuous and it's best not to think about it at all. Most days he is perfectly fine, but sometimes out there he fears being the monster because he looks different. How will people judge him? Will they flinch from him? For a while he wants to wear an eyepatch, to embrace his condition with an air of piratic bravado. But when his mother takes him to the shoe store in Yeoville, the women assistants say, 'Look at his long lashes and beautiful legs, I wish I had those,' which makes him feel like a girl. Or they talk of the 'beauty spot' below the corner of his eye, how they wish they had that too. The spot is lush and undamaged, and the comments bring complex feelings of pleasure and divorce. Maybe it would be nice to be a girl, though probably it's lucky he isn't, with that eye. Boys are allowed to be ugly, but he doesn't want to be.

Always, when it comes to his eye, there are the questions

demanding explanation, and he waits with a feeling of depletion for when he will be called on again to give another. Who hit you? What happened to *you*? Then he has to be a boy, and he ekes out a thin repertoire of responses. Why, what's wrong with it, I haven't noticed. Or, some boy did, but you should see him now (he had heard this somewhere, lame as it was). Later, he would get more inventive: my mother hit me with a frying pan. Or, often just quietly, it's a birthmark and it's permanent, which makes people cringe in shame—that is when they don't go on to explain that it's peculiar, because it looks *exactly* like a black eye.

By and large, people seem to accept him without noticing, or notice without saying anything, or whisper to one another without him seeing. Those polite ones, he sometimes wonders, what do they think happened to me—a question that never goes away. Spoken or unspoken, his eye is the great unsaid, unsayable in some ways. Here, in his early life, begins a daily lesson concerning the difference between appearance and reality, surface and depth, silence and speech. When people talk, gesture as well as language must be decoded, sound and tone are as important as words. He knows kindness when he feels it and unkindness when he doesn't. Most of all, he doesn't want to be misunderstood by what people see at first sight—or what he thinks they see. It is no accident that his underlying quest will be for depth, for meanings below the surface, for his mark is the very emblem of how surface misleads. No accident then that he has an excessively strong feeling for justice, especially in personal terms, and for time, which, if you are patient— and you have to be—will reveal the truth.

Close and far, left and right, girl and boy, body and mind. How to put the different aspects in tune?

15

All of this needs glossing, because it is more complicated. It was not simply true that I rejected surface, did not want people to notice it. In a way, I would divert attention to other kinds of surface—to humour, vitality, charm, or even (strangely) an engagement with the eyes, looking at them in a kind of dare. I wanted to be noticed in a certain way. In another life I might have made the most of this, become a rock star who did not have to paint his face to be different, start a cult. The real thing rather than its image.

At what point in my life did I begin to turn away from people on my right, not look there, or choose places to sit where I could look at people on my left with the minimum number on the right? Before I wore glasses I was unmasked, unmediated, bare, but after I got them they became a kind of shield, though logically I knew everyone could simply look through them. So, looking through them, I did not look, and did not want others to look at me. Glasses were my defence. Meet someone, eyes go down; I studied mouths rather than eyes. Wanting to be seen, I did not want to be seen. Such are the intricacies, the minute shifts by which on a grand scale the universe is governed. Or, what I mean is, imagine if that were how the universe is governed—how receptive we would be to the most intricate oscillations. Imagine if in the very first moments of time some of those proto-atomic particles had spun a little to the left rather than the right, where would we be now? Or if God had spoken in a slightly different tone, how different creation might be. The smallest ripples in time created galaxies; thus are the tiniest and vastest connected, that is how life takes on its shape.

At school I did well. Understanding and even copying (unusual for me, because drawing was not my forte) those mono- and di-cotyledon seeds, or the structure of teeth. Parsing sentences, to see how they worked. Geology with its aeons of time held a certain fascination. Just once there was an art project which seemed prophetic. We took a sheet of paper and covered it in wax crayon, all the colours of the rainbow, then covered that with another layer, of black. Then we took a pin and made line drawings in the black, removing it to reveal the colours below. Mine was a seascape with luminous fish and other wondrous creatures and a night sky of brilliant stars above. I loved the look of it, the whole bright spectrum emerging from the darkness. And at some level I loved the allegory. Beneath the layer of dark all the most beautiful colours of the world were waiting to appear, the miraculous essence underneath to be discovered in the most radiant shapes and lines. Without the dark there were no lines; without the markings no colours to be seen.

By the last year of primary school I was captain of both the soccer and cricket teams, and by coming second in everything in the inter-house athletic competition gained enough points to be victor ludorum (winner of the games—that was how we learned our Latin). At the beginning of the year I was named head prefect; mythology held that it was done by election, and there was indeed a vote, but later my father told me that the headmaster and teachers fixed it. It seemed that nothing I did could go wrong, and I felt the aura that others felt about me, almost embarrassed by it, wanting to be humble. Every year I won prizes; the great golfer Gary Player, who had been to our school, gave a cricket bat as an award, and I won it. In soccer I could do things almost at will on the field. For years I had been awarded school colours, wearing the special pocket on my blazer. Team photos at the end of each season marked my transitions—sturdy and tigerish when I was younger, leaner and more poised by the time I was twelve. Making a speech to thank the organisers at the end-of-year cricket tournament (when I was appointed vice-captain of the province), I spoke easily off the cuff, enjoying the spotlight. Only once did I miscalculate. I heard there was to be a fight on the school grounds, and as a prefect I should have put a stop to it. Instead I offered to referee it, and the cricket coach found me there, taking me to his office to be lectured on his disappointment and my shame. That was part of the news of the event, but there was another—the ambiguity of wanting to be different and wanting to be the same, to be visible in one way and invisible in another, just like everyone else in the crowd that had gathered round the boys.

I had good friends and played with them regularly, both at home and away. At one house I knocked a cricket ball through the front window, and there was the question of whether my parents should pay. Here I observed the reserved and almost cold atmosphere of one kind of non-Jewish family. When my friend told me that Jews have money, which was why my parents were rich, I responded that I couldn't help it if my father was smarter than his was. Early on I spent a lot of time with Daryl, whose father was our family doctor. They had a trellis at the back for their *sukkah*, with vines entwined around; we squeezed the exquisite purple Catawba grapes into our mouths from the skins. My friend David would come over often, and we'd steal my mother's cigarettes, trying them down at the bottom of the garden, feeling dizzy and sick; in Sandringham, where he lived, we'd sometimes buy them at one of the local shops. David's sister Debbie had polio as a child, and walked with callipers and crutches. Their parents had built a swimming pool for her to exercise, and she had amazing strength as well as an astonishing smile, determined as it was mysterious. In Sandringham another friend's mother died of breast cancer when we were about ten. The concept of breast cancer was as alien to me as the concept of death, and I did not grasp the meaning. But I do remember the house going very quiet afterwards, and later I felt guilty for not offering more understanding or compassion; I simply wasn't able to.

My friend Charl was an Afrikaner whose parents were probably Nationalists, but they had sent their son to an English-speaking school nonetheless. Charl was very smart, rumoured on occasion to be a genius, and one day after we took IQ tests teachers came round to our class just to look at him. At Charl's house I would see his grandmother, a diminutive and forbidding woman dressed in black whose mind always dwelt on the British concentration camps of the Boer War. If there were political tensions, they were unspoken; rules of politeness dictated otherwise. Still, in those years families like ours shared their pride in Helen Suzman, a Jewish woman who, with her sharp tongue and quick reflexes, was the lone hold-out in Parliament against the Nationalists, representing the Progressive Party. One year, during an election, we went past the school where someone had used the cricket scoreboard to register the fact that she had been in Parliament for thirteen years. The board read 'Suzman, 13 not out'.

One day as we came out of school to where the parents' cars were parked, there was a palpable feel of agitation in the air, and we heard the news that Prime Minister Verwoerd had been assassinated in Parliament. No one knew who had done it, but Charl's most courteous mother, in a rare show of passion, vowed that no matter how alone we were in the world, we'd stand up to our enemies and show them. The culprit turned out to be a Greek, a messenger (from the gods?) named Tsafendas, who had wielded the knife under orders, so he said later, of a tapeworm living in his stomach. But before that news emerged, it was ambivalence bordering on fear that was the greatest index of who we were. Verwoerd would not be missed, that much was clear, even if assassination was a rather stark way of getting rid of him. But what if the assassin had been Jewish? What if he had been black? We greeted Tsafendas almost with relief.

⌒ 16

Soccer lessons; and why trains are also trains of thought.

Inside-left is the facilitator position. It is your job to make things happen. You shuttle back and forth between the midfield and the forwards, and you also work left and right, linking both sides of the field. You are a playmaker, a kind of language in motion, generating the lines and combinations, a nodal point in the syntax of the team. As inside-forward you will sometimes score goals, and they may on occasion be spectacular, but your essential job is to make sure goals are scored, opening up the field to do so. I play on the left because I am so good with my left foot, but I can also come inside to use my right. Later I came to think of inside-left as not only a football position but also an ideological position; it has suited me well enough in either form. And it is a philosophical position as well: the game as language, the language as beauty, the inner music of its meaning and purpose. Time in a life is not like archaeology; at variable distances all layers are present at the same time, referring to and through one another. Who can say then what the present is, or the past?

Early on, when I was playing for my under-ten team, we went on a trip to Mooi River in Natal to play the school there. Of course it was winter, and we knew it would be cold, because Mooi River was close to the Drakensberg, which often had snow at that time of year. Before we left our coach came over to our house to borrow my father's overcoat; he didn't have one of his own. We travelled by train—the first time I had done so—six to a compartment in the sleeper coaches, three bunks on either side, their green-leathered upholstery made up with sheets and blankets for the night. In Mooi River I remember playing on a sand surface, but was it really that way? I think we won the game, and then on the Sunday evening everyone was meant to go to church in the town, a prospect that intimidated me no end. My parents, however, had spoken to the coach, and I was excused. Instead, he took me to an Indian restaurant (Indians had been settled in Natal since the nineteenth century). I think he too was mightily relieved not to have to go to church, and taking me out for a meal was some recompense for the coat. But just as I had never been on a train, so I had never been in a restaurant, let alone an Indian restaurant, and I had most certainly never eaten curry and rice. I didn't even know what a menu was, or what it was for, but soon worked it out, and there was some pleasure in that too. The meal was wonderful, the atmosphere of the place thoroughly convivial and warm. But on the train back I was on the lowest bunk, and all through the night I felt as if cascades of dust were descending on me, and I couldn't breathe. I came home with a raging fever, sick for days.

When I was eleven I went down to Natal by train again, this time with the Transvaal cricket team. I was a year or two younger than the other players, and didn't perform very well—a certain kind of reticence creeping in. I remember the team manager being surprised to hear my age, realising I would have another year to do better. Travelling down we were in the sleeper compartments again, and after supper in the lurching dining car, I felt like some chocolate. You couldn't eat on your own, and the only solution was to buy enough for everyone, which I did, magnanimously handing a few bars to a teammate to keep as we returned from the dining car to our compartment. Our team manager must have heard us go past, and came in to warn us to have a quiet night. As he left, sliding the door behind him, I turned to my teammate and 'Do you—' was all I could say (about to add '—have the chocolates?') when the team manager whipped back inside and demanded to know who had said that. Who had said what, we wanted to know. 'Someone swore at me,' he said. All I could think of was that he must have heard the 'do you' and believed it was something else, but I didn't own up. It was way too complicated, and in any case I didn't even know enough to imagine what he thought he might have heard. Still, he left us feeling chastened, and it took the edge off the chocolate experience. That night I woke to the sounds of murmuring and movement in one of the bunks; there were two boys up there, one saying to the other, no, don't put it here, put it there. In the morning I told them what I had heard, and they begged me not to tell anyone else. Later, some of the older boys in the compartment showed off their pubic hairs, but there was nothing for me to even think of showing. This is how knowledge comes, by paths both direct and indirect.

At sixteen I was on a train again, going down to Cape Town in December with friends for our first holiday away from parents, staying at a seedy hotel. By then we were already inured to our high-school experience, inaugurated for me some years before by the sight of two older boys clashing and thudding like two immense male kudu, doing their best to squeeze the life out of each other's testicles as they fought. Now in Cape Town there was a mix of innocence and edginess in the air, not least because on the streets and beaches as well as in other hotels girls roved in unaccustomed profusion. So you would find yourself in unspoken and anxious competition to look assured and competent around them, to behave with bravado and ease, something not easy for me because I was marked. On that trip we ventured in other ways, lining up to go serially into a pharmacy to ask for condoms which they kept behind the counter. There was no practical point in this; we just wanted to see what condoms looked like, and whether we would be able to get them. My friend Barry went in first and succeeded; I went in after and failed—the pharmacist clearly knew his customers. Then, on New Year's Eve, as the clock struck midnight, Barry seized hold of a beautiful girl in the tumult of the streets, kissing her passionately. She responded, and after what seemed a long while pulled away to say her boyfriend wouldn't like it. Barry asked, 'Where is your boyfriend?' and 'Right here!' said the boyfriend, who had arrived suddenly, whipping Barry around and cracking him full on the nose with his forehead—a technique known in the parlance as 'going him with the head'. It was a mad moment of timing, no more Barry's fault than ours, but now there he was in pain with his nose smashed. We got him back to the hotel where, for what was left of the seemingly endless night, he lay in the bunk above me and moaned while I was sure he was going to vomit all over me; we had all had a fair bit to drink.

At dawn we emerged from the hotel, Barry and I, trailing the roads of Sea Point, looking for an open chemist, or anyone who might help. Barry's nose was black and blue, as wide as his face, and we had hangovers to boot. Everything was closed, but a hobo pointed us towards a convent on a hill, saying they sometimes gave him soup. Accordingly, we tried the convent, but there they advised us to go to Woodstock Hospital. So we made our way to the central station, but on New Year's Day the trains were few and endlessly slow, and it took ages to get there. Woodstock was a notoriously rough part of town, and when we finally emerged from the hospital some hours later, all the toughs were out after their own challenging nights. But when Barry and I walked down the middle of the road, he with his nose, I with my black eye, like gunslingers in a Western, everyone parted for us like the Red Sea under the rod of Moses. Woodstock was near Newlands, the venue on New Year's Day for the traditional cricket match between Western Province and the Transvaal. So, with nothing else to do, we headed over to watch the cricket, and there it was the otherwise decorous and serene cricket spectators who parted for us, giving us a wide berth on the grass where we sat.

Later, back in school, it became apparent that Barry's nose had been badly treated in Cape Town, and would have to be reset. After the operation he had gauze up his nostrils—whole wads of it which he once showed us like a magician pulling endless ribbons out of a hat—and the doctors had told him to apply pressure to the side of his nose to correct what was now a notable bend. One day our Latin teacher was in one of his furies, berating us for some miserable failing, when he looked up to see Barry pressing the side of his nose with his forefinger. 'Bloody hell!' bellowed the Latin teacher, 'what the hell do you think you are doing?' 'Sir,' said Barry, 'I am straightening my nose,' at which point the classroom exploded.

17 ⤸

I feel dizzy with it all sometimes, sitting here in this quiet and peaceful house writing, doing my daily eye exercises which are also, inevitably, 'I' exercises. It was my father, equally inevitably, who first drew attention to the connection, by way of one of his endless observations. Of someone who couldn't stop talking about himself he would say, 'He has I trouble.' Is that what I have? Probably no more than anyone else, in a world where everyone has their own birthmarks.

So the boy—me, I, that boy over there in the distance—has begun to defer to the recognition and approval of others, especially those older than him. It is a relatively new but also growing pattern. At the age of seven I had decided for myself that I would get into the soccer team; no one had to approve. But by the time I was fifteen in high school, called out from class and told to attend cricket practices for the school first team, there was a change, and uncertainty was at war with belief. Now there was respect, too much respect, the wish for approval in the dialectic of visibility, not to stand out too much, not to offend. At practices the coach, an unctuous and overweening man who came to suppress my spirit almost entirely, would hit balls high, so much higher than I had ever seen them go, balls which seemed to rise into the very heavens and which, gathering unbelievable speed as they came down, you had to catch. My hands stung as never before; it felt vaguely sadomasochistic, and there was indeed a sexual undercurrent, because the coach, also the History master, sometimes

73

took a certain licence in class which everyone knew about. So there is strangeness in having been singled out, but at the same time I can't work out what will make this coach like me. The older boys, seventeen or eighteen, look at me with suspicion. Will I take one of their places? Ambivalence is theirs as it is mine; this is a new tightrope to walk, one I have not previously known.

The sexual world began early for me. When I was still quite small, my friend Gavin announced, without any invitation to do so, that he knew where babies came from, because his parents had told him. What strange parents were these, I wondered, who would discuss such a thing? Gavin passed on the information: babies came when mothers and fathers rubbed their wees together. It sounded thoroughly improbable, so improbable that we tried it, Gavin and I, in my bedroom at home under a kind of tent that we constructed from blankets. As far as I recall, it felt quite pleasurable, and later there were explorations with other boys which seemed at the time, and still seem, perfectly natural in a world that drove us to the clandestine. Yet I also remember from early on—when I was perhaps not much more than six or so—stopping while I was playing in the garden and sitting down quietly on the verandah steps because suddenly there was a strange stirring and hardening in my groin, and I had the feeling—which came from absolutely nowhere as far as I could tell—that I would like to be naked with a girl. I had no idea what to do with the feeling, and so just sat there until it passed. These things lived on together, boy and girl feelings, under the surface.

I did have early girlfriends, though. One lived on the corner of our road and Innes Street, and I would visit her there. At nursery school my girlfriend was Janet who lived on the ridge in Mountain View. Her father was an architect and the house had the most amazing glass frontage with sliding doors looking out on a breathtaking view over the northern suburbs. When I was ten, the sister of a cricket teammate became interested in me, and I found myself in love, writing her name in my schoolbooks, because that is what you are supposed to do, and going to visit her house. There one day another girl put a cricket protector over her face, asking if that was what it was for; though she knew exactly what it was for. Later still, it was the sister of yet another teammate who found a way to let me know she fancied me (the language of the time), and so I gravitated again, a new name making its way into my homework book. In these encounters I was strangely passive and pliant, acted upon rather than acting; yet I was also willing enough, because having a girlfriend was a bit like having an alibi. But I really didn't know what I wanted.

It was the edge between the perfect and fallen worlds. In the perfect world, pre-puberty, all was in balance. Later things changed and the world became confusing, as did everything in the mind, in the home. It worked in the way of any geology where one stratum rises towards the surface while another begins to fracture above it, but I can place one aspect of the movement quite precisely, in what is for me an eternal present tense. For this you have to understand the geography of our home in a literal and not metaphorical way. When you enter through our front door into the cool entrance hall with its dark polished brown tiles, on your left is the dining room and on your right the kitchen. On the far wall in the kitchen is an electric clock, ineffably modern. In the dining room are the beautiful Swedish table and chairs, and my place at the table is on the far side, so that looking through the door I can see through the entrance hall to the clock on the wall in the kitchen in the distance. It is always clear to me, so that I can easily tell the time, but one day something happens. A hand passes across my eyes, or someone flits briefly in front of me, and for that instant the clock blurs. It happens again, but I ignore it. Now and then, especially in the mornings, I have begun to be bothered by a mucous secretion in my right eye, relic of my operation, clouding my vision. I check for it, but that is not the cause this time, so I do a test. I put my hand over my left eye, and the clock is perfectly clear. I put my hand over my right eye, and the clock is blurred. It is a devastating feeling, and at first I won't believe it, but after a few experiments over some months I own up. Though I continue as I am for a while, eventually I am tested and the very year I enter high school will need glasses.

It may not seem much, but I am in the fallen world. The boy who lived through his senses and reflexes now looks through glass lenses. I am divided from the world, the split arriving with my growing-up and also sexual being. Left eye focuses close, right eye looks into the distance. Left, right, dark, light, girl, boy, now, then. Let's see: how do I look?

18

Across a world, across time, the cat has come in, and I observe her, simply because she is there to observe. If one can see the universe in a grain of sand, one can learn quite a bit from looking at a cat, not only about the present but the secret codes that speak through it of the past. Right now, for instance, her tail speaks even when she doesn't want it to. Normally, when she's walking down the path or coming into a room, she wears it straight and high behind her like a periscope. She is proud, she has a purpose, she is escorting us where we need to go, and the tail says it all. But now, having pinged on the door screen, she makes her way to the couch and begins to settle in. When I murmur to her or simply hum while I am reading my book, her tail starts to flap alongside her. If I speak to her directly, it starts to get worse. This is reflex, this is agitation. It makes her uneasy at this moment, the speaking. Can't you be quiet, it says, your words put me on the edge of what I can understand; I am flapping because this language of yours, these murmurs and noises, bother me. Seeing her flap like this, I stop, and gradually she looks more at ease. She puts a paw over her tail, now alongside her body, and settles her head on top of the paw. She looks to be going to sleep, but perhaps it is only pretence. The language of her tail has asked me to be quiet.

Where do these words come from? When I speak or write, it feels a bit like that tail to me, how it begins. There is a primal sensation, an inner shift of the slightest and almost imperceptible proportions, and yet it cannot be ignored. It is a bit like a compass, a sense of

77

direction, an instinct, an inner gesture starting deep down and eventually emerging into words. When I played soccer or cricket it was a bit like this, a physical reflex that spoke body into mind and then back into body again. I would see the players, the shapes, the spaces, gather an instantaneous sense of geometries, ratios, proportions, and in the midst of it feel a silence which I could fill in a certain way as my foot or bat connected with the ball, as if a word with a specific trajectory had been uttered, curving now through the air or scudding across the grass. What was I trying to say? I did not know, because the action was the word, in doing it I said it, it was its own kind of language.

Now, in conversation, when someone says something and I agree or object, I do so at levels far below anything I can at first communicate. Electric flash and jolt of the synapse: something, something there, pay attention. A shift inside, a reflex, what is it, movement, an inclination, no words yet, the point before the point, already there but what will it be, a mix of awareness and compulsion. I begin to make sounds, hazarded, risked, and now I am committed, and people begin to turn and look. The thought rises from the deeps in mind and body, and spirit lends its tone, and suddenly it is there in the mouth, on the tongue, about to launch into air. What am I going to say? I say it. I have said it. It is over, gone, un-unsayable, an event in the universe that can never be undone, though nothing at all can be undone, not even the smallest passing of the smallest nanosecond. The words echo, the spirit is still flapping. I put my paw on it to try to calm it down. Something has happened, something has been said, what did I say?

Everything happens at other levels, I am convinced of that, so that what comes to the surface is only the slightest expression of the impulses that prompted it. The most complex thoughts in the most profound of philosophers begin this way, as a tilting, a gesture, a signature, a something to say, let me find out what it is. When I was

78

growing up, our dog learned to open the glass door leading onto the verandah by pressing down on the handle. He was very adept, and would even open it for the other dogs when they wanted to go out. My father said his only problem was that he wouldn't shut the door again afterwards. But even those dogs were a kind of language, my father's secret, for where had they come from, why had we acquired three exquisitely beautiful but disturbing keeshonds who required such extensive care, and why was the one who could open doors called Billy of all things? Why such pompadourish specimens when all we ever had were mongrels and mutts? Deep down we all knew the answer, even though it was quite obscure and hard to formulate exactly. And who took care of the dogs but my mother, combing and brushing them with powder? It was all very strange, a language beneath language, one we could spend a good deal of time probing and decoding. Where do these words come from? They come, a flapping of tails, a periscope peering beneath the surface.

19

Sitting around the dinner table, with its classic oval shape and modern Scandinavian lines, we would hear my father say, 'When I was your age, I rode my bicycle from Orange Grove up Louis Botha hill without gears.' There was no doubt that my father had experienced hardships—the death of his older sister, his difficult relationship with his father, moving from house to house when he was young, staying with relatives. At this statement, we would predictably roll our eyes and joke. 'Yes, Dad, and you had to avoid the dinosaurs going up that hill as well.' But then he would retreat into his own kind of silence. There were things we did not understand about his life and never would, and he could not explain them either. What he had to explain lay some distance beneath anything about bicycles and gears; it had to do with his life, what he needed to explain, which was precisely why he couldn't do so.

My father had other stories that did correspond to feelings he could express. Like the time, when he was quite young, that he released the brake on a stopped tram at the intersection of Bedford Avenue and Louis Botha, opposite the primary school. He had seen the driver do it a million times, but now the driver had gone off into a shop to buy something, and the passengers on the tram were waiting for him to return. My father was alert, he could see something and know how to do it, so he said to his friend, 'Watch this'—or some equivalent—jumped up and ran to the driver's area where he released the lever that controlled the brake. The tram started moving towards the intersection, but my father didn't know how to put the brake on again. Panic was rising when at the last second the driver jumped back on and brought the tram to a halt. He took my father's name and address, and my father said he was too scared even to lie. Thereafter, for a period of about six months, whenever the front doorbell rang, he made himself scarce. Stories like this made us laugh, no matter how many times we heard them. This was my father being light about himself, but also a little proud, and we adopted some of that pride too—the pride in the instinctive, the reflexes, the coordination of body and mind that could allow you to observe, in the first place; absorb, in the second; and then jump instantly into action.

We had our bicycles, of course, and they had gears, though not many. For me it was my beloved straight-handled bike with the Sturmey-Archer gears (three-speed) which I would ride round and round the yard, making Johanna and Stevens giddy. It felt made for me, as I was for it. Or I would ride like a maniac down the side of the house, onto the front lawn (we called it the front, even though it was at the back), down the embankment onto a raised quadrangle of lawn on the other side of the jacaranda, and launch myself into space as I flew off it like a ski-jump. My brother's bike had drop handlebars and derailleur gears (five), and once, hitting something in the street, he did a somersault over the handlebars and chipped his front teeth. He it was who taught me how to ride, on the road outside our house, where the hill went down Mons towards Innes. He put me on the saddle, wheeled me around a bit, and then simply pushed me off. By the time I got to the bottom of the hill I could ride. It was crude, and I was petrified as I sailed off down the small hill, but it was effective; I didn't know whether to feel outraged or grateful.

It was only years later that I registered the echoes of my mother's bicycle stories, though of course I had heard them before. She would say, 'When I was small I just loved my bicycle,' and 'I was on my bicycle all the time.' She spoke about the veld in the small, rural town of Kempton Park where they lived, and then she would say, 'Sometimes I would just get on my bicycle and ride to Benoni.' How far away was that? 'About nine miles.' And how old were you? 'I would have been about ten.' So, at the age of ten my mother would have taken off on a bicycle (without gears) to ride the eighteen miles to Benoni and back, and would have done it without telling her mother or father. Once, she said, she rode her older sister Sheila's bike, but it was too big for her, and perched on the saddle she couldn't reach the foot brakes. She ended up crashing into a fence at the railway station, anxious—as always with my mother—not about herself but the damage she might have done to her sister's bicycle.

She had other stories too. Of sharing that room with her grand-mother, who slept with one eye open. Of seeing Africans in the third-class carriages on the train and asking her mother, at the age of three or four, why they were treated so badly. Of waking her sister Sheila in the early hours every night to take her to her mother's bed. Of wishing, more than anything else as a child, that everyone in her whole family could sleep in one bed, so that no one would be left out. Of worrying, if that were to happen, about who would have to sleep on the outer edges. There were chickens and cats everywhere, the outhouse they all had to use—her fear of unsanitary things ever since, her nose the finest working organ in her body. When my mother was small, the last of four girls, her mother cut her hair short for a while and they called her 'Jimmy'. When she travelled on her own by train to school in Germiston every day, she would see the Greyshirts and hear them talking about the Jews. She, on her own, stood up to them: 'I am Jewish,' she said. When, many years later, she saw me hugging our younger daughter on a bench at the Zoo Lake in Johannesburg, she told me her own father had never hugged her. But when they went driving, it was she who gave her father directions; she noticed everything, he told her, and she did.

Adults in our world—at least white adults—did not ride bicycles, and so my mother would have given it up, much as she gave up a lot she loved doing to live in the world she inhabited. It was simply the way things were done, and she, always worried about not offending, conformed. She lost touch with her own physical instincts. She gave up tennis, which she also loved, and orchestrated lunches for my father's family on Sundays. She gave up dancing, because that was something my father didn't like. She gave up her work—her beloved market research—when my father began to make money and he insisted. Later came the difficult times, which both she and my father had to face, and then she alone. There was the broken ankle, the replaced hip, the growing deafness, facing uncertain times.

All through her life my mother never learned how to swim, because her father said the dam in Kempton Park was too dangerous. Everyone always told her what she could not do. But inside her is that other mother, the person I have been thinking of, the one I still see, who laughs infectiously, cares for everyone, and writes the most feeling of notes. She is the one who never lost contact with her instincts or the ability to enact them. She is light on her toes and on her feet; she has taken to dancing again, she goes out to do market research with her beloved actress-friend Wena Naudé and with Faye who used to fry fish in the nude. She can ride to Benoni and back without telling anyone, stand up to the Nazis on the train before nonchalantly alighting, survive a crash into a fence and get up defiantly to go ride some more. She likes rides in the countryside, she does not bother about what other people think, she is content in herself, gliding serenely into the future.

⌒ 20

Once, in primary school, we ventured out on a field trip of sorts. We didn't go far, but marched two-by-two in our green blazers and small-peaked caps and ties, out beyond the swimming pool into Oak Lane, and then towards Munro Drive. From here, looking out over the canopy of purple jacarandas in the northern suburbs, on a good day you could see the Magaliesberg mountains on the horizon. The object of this trip, however, was not scenery but geology. For Munro Drive had been carved out—blasted out, probably—from one of the ridges that striated Johannesburg, rocks and outcrops glistening in the sun. What you could see along the cliffs of Munro Drive, particularly on the first steep curve going down, was strata—exposed strata of rock layered through the ages. Mostly the strata were horizontal, but here and there sharp angularities interrupted where upheavals had occurred.

We touched the rocks, palms to warm stone. Feel it, see it in a new way. Look out into the distance. This is a place of space and time, time reaching back, space reaching forward. Where had it come from, where was it turning? It was Africa, sure enough, but just a glimpse of it, a hint, a sensation of what might be, of what had been, mostly tamed in our lives, but revealed here as an intimation, a different way of seeing our surroundings. This was our place, becoming our city, but it had other stories going back and back, underlying everything we took for granted. Just a hint here, a glimpse there, the taste of stone on the fingers. What would

84

it take to see this every day, to live in this light, in this rock, in this air, under these stars? To see the people who had lived here long ago, to really see their descendants? Underneath my life was something unknown, like the tremors we felt at night in our beds, as the earth, mined out for gold, gave way somewhere, and the slow reverberating rumble would shake the floors and walls, the underworld risen to the surface, measured in the deep vibrations of our bones.

Whenever we went on holiday—which was not that often—we would wake early, around three in the morning. The world, still dark, swung around outside. Clothes on quickly, excitement almost unbearable, tea and toast in the kitchen, luggage loaded in the car, and then we would drive off, the sun rising somewhere along the way. These were our lives upside down, and never more alive than in such rituals. We would sit in the back of the car, half sleepy, half wide awake, taking it all in, the sillhouetted hills and grasses along the road slowly merging into the colours of day. One morning, travelling down the new dual-lane highway towards Cape Town, for no reason at all I said, wouldn't it be funny if a car came the other way towards us on the wrong side of the road? And then, as we crested a hill, a car came the other way towards us, on the wrong side of the road. Much further down that road, the semi-desert of the Karoo presented its stark and extraordinary beauty.

One year we went to Bushman Rock in the Eastern Transvaal, a road trip with magical names: Tzaneen, White River, Phalaborwa, Magoebaskloof. We stopped at a stream where water poured over a weir. My father said, 'A weir is like a sieve—like so-and-so's brain' (his constant joke, usually about memory). At Bushman Rock we stayed in a hotel owned by a man he had known from the Air Force. It was built into the very rock of the outcrop where it stood, and carved out of the rock was the most remarkable swimming pool, not with straight sides and lines but curves following the flow of the granite. There you could leap across the boulders like a rock rabbit, off to where the bushman paintings were concealed in a steep bat-fluttering cleft, just squeezing in to see the images. The man who owned the hotel had a daughter, slightly older than I, named Sigrid; I had never heard the name, and turned it into 'cigarette' in my mind. She was long, lithe, boyish and beautiful, and I fell in love. We swam together in the pool, lay like lizards on the warm rocks to dry. My father almost never swam, but there he came in a striped swimming suit, like a wild man rising out of the water with his black hair hanging over his eyes.

Once when I was small, before I could swim, I jumped into an empty swimming pool believing my father would catch me because he had been there just before in the water while I leaped; he jumped in again to save me. When I was fourteen I went with my uncle Stanley and aunt Valerie on a trip to the game reserve in the Kruger National Park, one of the happiest times. That sense of the lowveld as we travelled, and then the park itself: all I can picture are dawn and evening silhouettes, the feel of the sun, the red earth and smell of the grass, the stars at night, the sounds of the birds, all its own form of being whether with us or without us. One winter, when we were sixteen, I went camping with my friend Barry in Botswana, along with my girlfriend's brother-in-law. We lay in a culvert downwind from a herd of elephants, and constructed a ring of spiked doringboom branches around our tent at night; the brother-in-law had heard a lion or a cheetah, and insisted that *he* would sleep in the car. We drank boiling-hot coffee in the bitter cold of the early mornings. Barry spilled boiling water on my fingers; I didn't feel a thing.

This was the earth, the African earth, but in Cape Town there was a different sensation. There one evening I leaned over the parapet in Kalk Bay gazing at the ocean as the day turned to twi-light and then to darkness. Here were the waves coming in, and as they rose and moved towards the rock and the parapet, coming and coming again, my breathing fell into rhythm with their rising and falling. I felt the depth, the time of it, the swell and suck and shudder and release of it, always gathering and gathering again. I was wholly in and out of myself in that motion of rising and falling, seeing in a way that went beyond seeing because it was a kind of not-knowing where I was, how I was, merely that I was, there in that moment on the parapet between earth and water, rising and falling towards the water as I stood, breathing in and out as I breathed, like the waves rising and falling forever in that place.

In that moment I felt those rhythms inside me. The land was time, the sea was eternity. One was here, the other everywhere; one was now, the other always. One wanted me to stay, the other beckoned me away. Somewhere between the bright intimations of land and the deep eternities of ocean my spirit drifted and flew, seeking its own kind of home.

⟅ 21

The apple hangs in the air as if all time and space have been suspended. There it hangs, light glinting off its polished surface, and everyone gazing at it is suspended too, watching the apple intently, but also frozen because something else is happening across the room. What that something else is: a foot in the door. Our Maths teacher has arrived and is about to enter the room. Soon she will see it all: us, the commotion, the bodies frozen in movement, and the apple, she will see that too, in the next instant. That is why it is suspended there, as if taunting us with the inevitable workings of time. My friend Colin has thrown it, the climax to a sequence of utter pandemonium, because although the bell rang ten minutes ago, the teacher has not yet arrived. But now she has arrived, and as she enters and absorbs the scene, and as the noise dwindles into silence, suddenly time starts to move again, and the green apple, speeding ruthlessly on its way, smashes into a framed picture on the far wall, mis-timed, mis-aimed, and the glass shatters into splinters.

We were that sort of class, in that sort of school: the 'A' class, meant to be better, but also in uproar in a high school that did its best to subdue us. Accordingly, things happened. In science class the teacher does not arrive, so we climb out of the window and make our way down to the swimming pool on the other side of the school grounds. When we are discovered we are taken to the headmaster, who bends us over and canes us. One of our science teachers, dressed in his perpetual white lab coat, has a scalp that seems to lift up and down in a kind of reflex from his ears to the top of his head. Another seems to go into a trance whenever someone asks him a question, and naturally the questions multiply. A boy brings in a tennis ball: with the teacher in his other-worldly state, he throws the ball against the wall behind him. Teacher hears the sound and whips round, cartoonlike, but the ball has already bounced back beyond him, so he misses it. Or he does an experiment, showing us how an electric current creates a magnetic field which you can measure with a compass. But one of the boys puts a magnet up his sleeve and waves it over the compass so that the needle goes round and round, and the teacher goes off into a trance again. The teacher brings in a cane to create the appropriate feeling of awe, but when he is not looking a boy takes the cane and breaks it in two, throwing the pieces out of the window. Teacher brings in another cane, with exactly the same result: this is its own form of science, verification through repetition. Later, in History class, a boy sitting in the front row next to the window jumps out of it when the teacher turns his back to write notes on the board for us to copy. When the teacher turns around, he says he could have sworn the boy was there. By the time he turns around again, the boy has come back through the window. Teacher later has a heart attack, and we all feel suitably guilty.

As we should have. But there was that business of writing notes up on the board for us to copy verbatim and repeat in exams. No wonder we had to make our own amusement. One of our teachers, dressed impeccably in a pin-striped suit, read directly to us out of our abysmal history textbook (all those unscrupulous whites who sold arms to the blacks in the nineteenth century), insisting we keep our copies closed so that we couldn't simply read along with him. As we learned about the Great Trek and the Boer War and its nine causes for the umpteenth time, he told us that the British concentration camps weren't intended to kill, but what could they do about disease? He knew this, because his grandfather had been commandant of one such camp. There was that other History teacher, the cricket coach, who would wander around the class putting his hands on the boys' backs and necks, and sometimes down their shirts, no doubt some form of Platonic ritual. One teacher—the inevitable guidance teacher—was also a cricket coach, and commented appreciatively on my legs and backside at practice as I bowled. He used to amuse us in class by putting a piece of chalk like a cigarette vertically on his tongue, closing his mouth around it, and then opening up to uncurl it again. At a practice when I was batting, a ball hit me high up on the inside of my thigh, which made the teacher run up and rub me under my shorts, right there in front of everyone. He also suggested I come back with him to his rooms in one of the boarding houses where he had some cream he could apply, but I demurred. Some time later he left precipitately, the rumour was for having one of the second-team rugby wings in his bed.

Later, some of us felt that all our lessons about politics in South Africa were learned in that school—through a kind of direct experiential method. Did you want to know about colonialism? Look no further: our school was the exemplum. How about corruption? The instances multiplied. Racism wasn't exactly required, because under apartheid there were no blacks at our school. But being Jewish? Ah, that was another matter. All of it was conducted with perfect decorum, so you could scarcely say what was real and what not, but by the end it felt real enough. The boy who went through it knows about it, because things happened and didn't happen to him directly, so that by the time he left he was more or less depressed. He vowed to study History, because there had to be more to it than the drivel they had to digest. He decided that if he ever wrote enough books, he would dedicate one to the cricket master whose hands went down shirts, because he gave him the incentive just to go on and find his own way. That is what schools are for: part of your education is surviving some of your teachers.

But light did come, and for me it was in my Latin class, of all unpredictable things. For there we had a teacher (we called him Hughie) who made us think, who taught us the sublimities of Greek mythology along with our grammar, so that we knew its landscape of heaven and earth like the stairs we climbed every day to his room. He gave us the saucier poems of Catullus to read, and asked us, when we saw the word *vaginam* in a passage of Caesar, to decode from the context what it meant (answer: a sheath for a sword, in the accusative form, which tells you something about the Roman view of both martial matters and sex). He, rumoured to be gay like some of the other masters, put no hands down anyone's shirt. He it was who, in our final year, had us perform Sophocles' *Antigone* with its lessons of the laws of God and the laws of men, its intrinsic advice on how to live under an unjust regime, perspective enough for both school and country. He it was who, for the essay section of our final exams, gave us no topic but only a photograph of an American tank in Vietnam pulling a dead enemy soldier in the dust by his ankle on the end of a rope. The reference was to Achilles dragging the body of Hector around the walls of Troy against every human law of decency, and it was also to the United States and South Africa, my present and future homes, an image to haunt always.

Rehearsing *Antigone*, some of the boys read the lines of the chorus in black South African accents. Easy—far too easy—to re-enact the wider world we came from, even if in satirical jest. But were those voices also the absent world paying us a visit? Ours was a doubly segregated school, no girls as well as no blacks, and when we performed the play, my friend David took the title role and looked, so to speak, rather austere. Our friend Clive played her sister Ismene and, like his own sisters, looked positively gorgeous. I was the short-skirted Haemon advising his father Creon, fruitlessly, to be more flexible in imposing his destructive impetuosity and will.

☞ 22

I sit on the windowsill, light streaming through, polishing my brother's cadet boots and the brass of his shoulder badges, listening to Bob Dylan singing 'Sad-Eyed Lady of the Lowlands' from *Blonde on Blonde*. It is an incongruous combination, but there is something in the plaintive chords that seems filled with an ineffable and beautiful longing, and perhaps the repetitive nature of my activity provides just enough focus for inward contemplation. When not cleaning the boots or whitening my brother's puttees, I take out John Fowles's *The Magus*, with its air of romance and mystery, and read it while listening to 'Sad-Eyed Lady' yet again. The record player is a single-piece affair, with a top that detaches to become a rather tinny-sounding speaker. But it is an advance over those old gramophones with needles you had to insert, and the sheer magic of being able to listen to music like this speaks to my soul. We are part of a new world of youth, even in South Africa, and its sounds invite immersion and surrender. I have been into the centre of Johannesburg to a music store with my friend Barry and heard The Band play *Music from Big Pink* in one of the audio booths, where the bass reverberates right through your body. Robbie Robertson's guitar lines tell a plaintive story on their own. The world is transforming, and our sensibilities are testing, being tested, as we change with it.

In this world I went to my first parties, the anxiety around my eye counteracted—or reinforced—by the see-through aubergine shirt and mustard corduroy pants I was wearing. I had no idea what to do, how to behave, but actually managed to speak to some girls. There was mystery, and a secret, and everyone else seemed to know the answer, but all I could do was summon up my courage and brazen it out. Later on in high school, on Saturday nights, we went hitchhiking all over Johannesburg, way into the depths of the northern suburbs, arriving at parties to which we had been invited and gatecrashing those to which we had not. Sometimes we would go to three or four parties in a row, and there were a number of miracles associated with this. One was that anyone at all would give us lifts as we put out our thumbs in groups of up to four or five. Another was that our parents seemed to allow it, or at least allow themselves to be willingly deceived. For there was serious deception in the air. When I arrived home late on a Saturday night, or when my mother asked me the next day, it was always some friend's father who had given us a lift, or the father of a friend of a friend. (Why, my parents might have wondered, were they never the ones to give the lift; or perhaps we did ask them from time to time, just to maintain credibility.) Strangely it was, in its own way, a golden age of physical freedom, at least for teenage white boys, and some girls, in Johannesburg, even if, underneath it all, the spirit sometimes asked its nagging questions: what was it all about? Decades later and we would barely have been able to leave the house without an escort or buzzers at the ready for the armed response services when we returned home. Our parents may have been deceived, but at least they got some sleep.

I might have cleaned my brother's cadet boots as a favour—not because my brother asked me—but why did I do it? Still a mystery. Yet I was not so good at cleaning my own. In fact by the time I had to do so on a regular basis, I hated the idea of cadets and what it stood for so much that the thought left me somewhere between lassitude and repugnance. On many a cadet day when we had to wear the military uniform to school I looked little more than dissolute, as if I had come out of a particularly rough night. That little piece of sprung machinery to put under your collar to keep it straight and pointed, the puttees, the boots—it all seemed simply ridiculous, let alone marching to the constricted nasal wail of bagpipes (in hell a kilted bagpipe band awaits me). It was a mindless and utterly futile militarism. Even without the distant sense of the apartheid army ahead of us, I objected on the instincts of a response that was aesthetic and philosophical (all of it inchoate, all of it some way beneath articulation) as much as it was political.

And there were the rituals. Every year on 11 November, we observed Armistice Day, with a ceremony in the school quadrangle around the phallic plinth that rose in its centre, with the names of former schoolboys who had died in the service of their country. My brother was a guard command officer (gleaming sword held up, handle to the point of his nose), the regular preface to becoming a prefect, but when my turn came I was unable to conform to the code. The teacher in charge was a former head prefect who had come back to school to teach Geography, offering us monotonous lessons on sheep farming in Australia. He also made our class draw the most meticulous maps of Africa, not a bad thing in principle, but one of our tasks was to draw the Cape-to-Cairo railway. In groups we pored over atlases and reference books with gathering panic because we couldn't find it, and finally in perplexity delivered the message to the teacher: 'Sir, there doesn't seem to be a Cape-to-Cairo railway.' 'Well,' came the answer, 'if there isn't one, you can't draw it'—and of course there wasn't. The projects we delivered to this teacher would later be found in the dump near one of the boarding houses where he was a master, otherwise untouched and unmarked, which didn't prevent him from giving us grades for them at the end of term. From time to time we'd see him flying kites on one of the rugby fields.

94

On this particular day he wasn't impressed, because my uniform was in disarray, and the same was true for many others in our platoon as we lined up. One thing about this teacher, however, was that he hadn't quite grasped the mechanics of our school—something he should have known better. Or perhaps he was a reformer, because instead of the usual method of choosing the guard command, which was what he was doing that day, he must have decided to judge everyone on merit. Or what he conceived of as merit, which basically meant how your brass shone and how white your puttees were. So, in increasing fury, he pulled us out one by one, and I was discarded. But I was also destined to be a prefect, which caused some consternation in the symbolic system of the school. Guard command officers will be prefects, and vice versa. Oh my, what are we to do now? Well, it really didn't matter to me at all. And so I am no guard command officer, and as our English teacher would say, who can care? (We translate it into ridiculous Latin: *quis curare potest.*) Later I would sustain my one-person refusenik form of military resistance, whereas the Geography teacher became an official in the apartheid-era South African embassy in Australia, serving as a spokesperson when a woman named Kirsti Valiaho was beaten with a broom handle by one of his fellow diplomats during a demonstration marking the tenth anniversary of the Soweto Uprising.

⌒ 23

In Form Two, when we are fourteen, the headmaster comes into the classroom and announces that he has seen the future. He has been to America, and the future, he tells us, is in computers, but he pronounces the word in the American way, as 'com-*pu*-ders'. We are the 'A' class, and should pay attention, but none of us takes it seriously, which elicits a visible sense of despair in the headmaster. None of us, that is, except Derek, who goes on later to write a software program and make his fortune. The class the headmaster has come into is our Latin teacher's—not our usual Hughie, but an Italian woman who makes us use Italian pronunciation, with 'ch' sounds (as in 'church') for *c*'s and soft *g*'s, so that we say 'Jermania' instead of Germania, which will later drive Hughie mad. '*Silencio!*' she shouts at us, insisting that we boys sit with our knees together, because it is disgusting for her to have to look at us in front of her with our legs splayed. This is unlike our guidance teacher, who sits on her desk in front of us with all *but* her legs splayed, her short skirt drifting up her stockings towards her waist. Guidance like that is guidance we can appreciate, and for once there is competition to sit in the front row in class.

Our Afrikaans teachers are a strange bunch, and we have a plentiful supply of them. One of them, large and bulbous, is called 'The Blob', and has a fearful reputation. Rumour has it that he sometimes kicks the lintel above his classroom door on the way in, or brings a pellet gun to shoot at the mice scurrying around the floorboards at the back. Our industrial arts teachers are always Afrikaners, perpetually boiling with barely suppressed rage at the overprivileged *Engelse kêrels* they have been fated to teach. One of the woodwork teachers is particularly brutal. When we have to draw plans of the objects we are about to construct (bookends, a tray), his instructions are given in a heavy accent, hard to follow. Did he say a thin line, but not too thin, thick but not too thick, bold but not too bold? We mock him: draw a thin thick straight curvy strong wobbly line. Once when I am talking as, through rictal jaws, he burbles out his directions, he calls me out, bends me over and hits me with a plank—an item in plentiful supply in a woodwork class. It really hurts—much worse than straight caning. I am useless in these subjects, and it takes me a while to learn how to survive. In metalwork, along with some of my classmates, I get my friend Matthew to finish the trowel I am making. In art, where I habitually get an 'E', eventually I stop handing in work altogether and get a 'C'—a sign, I believe, of my teacher's gratitude and relief, a secret understanding.

One of our Afrikaans teachers is also our rugby coach, and he tells us with supreme confidence that when we play Helpmekaar, the Afrikaans school, '*hulle gaan julle moor*'—'they are going to murder you'—because this is a man's game that you English boys are just too lilylivered to play. No use fussing about it, it is just a fact of life. We take to the field in trepidation, expecting not only to be beaten but to be beaten up, for we have heard that these Helpmekaar players wear aluminium studs in their boots and have no compunction about using them in the rucks when the referee can't see. But in the end we win quite handily, which embarrasses our teacher no end, and I even have a hand in it, surprising myself by selling a dummy pass to an opposing player, and then sending off one of my teammates to score under the posts. Generally, I hate rugby; in South Africa it is an ideological game, meant to turn us into white men when we get to high school. After primary school I constantly mourn the loss of soccer, but according to the world we live in that game is for blacks or presexual white boys when they might as well be girls. British colonial and Afrikaner nationalist cultures mesh, and the net result is that we are doomed to the hammering world of rugby.

There is a woman who teaches us Afrikaans whose fits of rage cannot be stifled. Once, marching over to the open door of the classroom, she calls us nothing better than a bunch of *kaffers*—she uses the Afrikaans pronunciation for the dreaded, unsayable word. As she slams the door shut towards her, the handle comes off in her hand and she staggers back towards her desk. A superannuated teacher who appears to be suffering from incipient Alzheimer's (though no one knows the word then) lectures us on how illogical English is compared with Afrikaans. In Afrikaans, when you give an address, *first* you give the street name, *then* you give the number—the way you would find it if you actually made the trip. But in English, first you give the number, then the street, completely backwards; this seems to him a decisive illustration. In these classes we learn endless idiomatic expressions: to speak nonsense is (in Afrikaans) 'to speak English', to be drunk is to be 'high in the branches', to be exhausted is to be '*vier bene in die lug*'—four legs in the air, but we mistranslate it as four beans in the light. Our form of resistance is to pronounce it all in the most plummy of Anglo accents, which further enrages our teachers, for style and sound, like rugby, are ideology and nationality, and in both respects we are clearly suspect.

If there is brutality and weirdness, there is also a surprising amount of sentimentality; the two are strangely entwined in these teachers. It is a sentimentality to which I am not immune, and when we read a book called *Vlekkie*, about the inevitable dog who goes missing but is eventually reunited with the boy who loves him, tears come to my eyes. 'Vlekkie' means the equivalent of 'Spot' (or mark), and I believe he has one under his eye, but this is not the only reason I see myself in the story of the dog, in this tale of loss and return. My right eye weeps all on its own, as it often does whether in wind or currents of emotion, and I can't control it. When the teacher looks up and sees me overflowing quietly at the back of the classroom, he says, '*Ja, Clingman, wat huil jy?*' ('why are you crying?'). But there is kindness as well as amusement in his voice, and as the rest of the class turns round to witness me, I sense not cruelty but silent understanding, which must mean they are secretly feeling something as well.

Guidance teachers will tell us about Moses leading his people out of Egypt, and one of them doesn't know whether to call them 'Israelis' or 'Isra-laai-tees'. But is any of this worse than the suffusion of Anglo colonial hypocrisy that seeps into every brick of the school? And not only there. Down the road is St John's, a private Anglican school, and when we cross over to play rugby or cricket, I know I am definitely not wanted. No one says anything of course, but it is almost as if there is a huge sign hanging over the school saying 'Jews Not Particularly Encouraged'. Within those precincts the temperature drops appreciably, and the sky grows dimmer; I just cannot do what I am supposed to in the chill air. It is the same at private schools in Natal when we travel down to play cricket, where they will say Christian prayers before supper and have only pork on the menu. It's hard to bat well after that. Once, at St John's when I am fourteen and playing rugby, one of the opposing players puts out a foot and pushes me over it with all his might. The odd thing is that I didn't even have the ball, no comfort as I went flying through the air to land on my shoulder and break my right collarbone. Of course I didn't know it immediately, and tried to play on for a while, but when the St John's referee came over to where I was lying on the ground, I said, 'Jesus Christ, he tripped me.' 'No need to bring *Him* into it,' he said, before giving us a free kick.

⌒ 24

There is a hole in the fence where I can get through in the mornings.
Of course we aren't supposed to, because it is an undignified procedure, beneath the acceptable standards of a school such as ours,
but at a certain place the iron railings are broken, and one can just
about squeeze in. This is the back entrance to the school, or one
of them, near the cricket nets and the boarding houses, and it cuts
out the extra seven to ten minutes it would take to proceed via the
proper and more decorous way. But at this stage in my life I am
always late, even though I am a prefect, and being on time is not one
of my priorities. What are my priorities at this stage? I don't know, it
is a mystery to me; I seem to have lost my way, so back routes are as
serviceable as any other.

Before, at primary school, when we sang 'All Things Bright and
Beautiful', the most cheerful of the Christian hymns for assembly,
I would be up early, trying as hard as I could to be the first boy to
arrive in the morning. My father got into the spirit of it too, waking
me early as I requested. I never quite made it—to be first, that is—
but there I would be crossing the road at the gates, tipping my cap
(as taught) to the drivers who allowed me through, and entering
the school past the bicycle shed. At a certain stage in high school
I would bike in, careering with my cricket bag swinging wildly—
beware a bat handle in the spokes—and swerving in to park in the
gothic space under the school buildings. There you would ascend the
stone stairs to the noticeboards at the top near the quadrangle. The

remembered details emerge only in unpleasant dreams, for at these boards I will learn again and again just what the order of things is at the school.

When I was ten or twelve, my father would drop me off on his way to work. He would call to wake me up, I would bolt down my breakfast, and we would leave in the car. At Louis Botha Avenue, which we had to merge with and cross quickly, my father would push combatively into the heavy traffic, virtually forcing drivers to let him in. There I heard language of a richer kind. 'You bastard,' he would offer under his breath, or, louder, 'Yes, and you too, you s-h-one-t,' or 'I've got a soft spot for you and you can kiss it!' Were all fathers like this? Couldn't he just take it easy sometimes?

Now I don't get a lift, nor do I ride a bike, but I walk, that is to say run, because I am habitually late. I have my shortcuts, know every last move down Mons Road to St Peter's and Cavendish, crossing Louis Botha to the back road alongside the cricket fields, and in through the hole in the fence. I will see other laggards doing the same thing, boys I should, as a prefect, reprimand for being late, but I too am late, and we are all scrambling like hell so we can skid into assembly and I can take up my place, ostensibly to conduct the surveillance of others but really to pay no attention at all as the day begins. After a while I abandon my place in the prefects' room, where I was once caned in the most peculiar circumstances. That doesn't matter now; it is the atmospherics of the room that repel me, the ethos of stunted male malevolence, the swagger of shoulders, the creation of identity in an invented self-belief. Minds are wholly in service to the body; this is how we become who we are in the regime of the school.

Against this, my friends and I continue to fashion a life for ourselves. On the last day of every term we gather at Johnny's house in Lower Houghton for soccer or swimming or just hanging around. There I hear Cream for the first time, and Jimi Hendrix, and Procol

Harum. I ride my bike to Johnny's, or to my friend Clive, going down the S-curves of Munro Drive with the tree-lined avenues laid out below, and back up the steep incline again when I go home. There I can retrace the path my father always took at speed in the car, thrilling and terrifying the boys in the back as he brought them home from a cricket match, brushing the stone-lined walls with just inches to spare. My father's judgement for all things physical was nothing if not acute.

In school, things happened on the edge of the customary world. One of my friends brought in pictures of a man and a woman ranged on furniture having sex. Because the whole concept was unaccustomed, I couldn't make sense of it at first, the positive and negative space, the woman with dark stockings and white skin and dark fur, the stark blacks and whites of the images. What in these obscure pictures was what? Were they upside down over there? You had to pretend, but it was perhaps one of the other boys in the class, ridiculed for being uninterested, who was more honest about the strangeness he was confronting.

There was also a boy named Louis who was a bit different. He seemed to be in a world of his own, with just the hint of an inward smile always on his face. Once, when he was caught for something or other, he was given lines to write out, but when we looked in his book, all we saw were rows and rows of meaningless squiggles. The teacher saw it too, and didn't comment; I think we must all have admired it just a bit. At some point Louis admitted that he wanted to be a ballet dancer, which seemed unlikely because he appeared if anything a little ungainly, and in any case the concept of ballet for boys was virtually unimaginable, though sometimes I secretly thought of myself as a dancer. One day, coming in fairly late to school, this time by the more conventional route, I passed the rugby fields, where the stands lined the first-team pitch. The place was vacant, for the first bell must have rung—just long enough to hurry to be in time. But there, on the top row of the stands, I saw Louis, alone and oblivious to all else, pirouetting on one leg, arms flung out at the shoulders, knee bent out to the side in not quite perfect form. He spun round and round, not minding, perhaps not knowing, he would be late. He was playing to the empty space on his stage; instead of watching rugby from the stands, the rugby fields were watching *him*. Years later I saw someone with his name in a ballet performance at the Civic Centre in Johannesburg, not as one of the main dancers but in the corps. I still don't know if it was him, but the image of Louis pirouetting on the empty stands at the school remained an emblem in my mind. Strange as it was, his gesture represented a radical freedom, a simple refusal to care what the world thought. For my part, I seemed to be waiting for something to happen, yet had no idea what it was. How would one get there, through which hole in which fence?

⌒ 25

Going into a sandwich shop in Johannesburg, near the university, I saw a woman behind the counter who looked at me and said cheerfully, 'Oh, you have a birthmark under your eye.' Taken aback for a moment, I told her it was remarkable. She was the first stranger I had met who had known right away what it was—and had said so, very pleasantly. She said it was no mystery, because her son had exactly the same marking, except that it was under the other eye. I was amazed. So there were at least two of us in the world; we made a pair, her son and I, symmetrical left and right. Was that a better or worse feeling? I was no longer so distinctive.

I thought perhaps we could form a society. But what would it be called, and how far would it go? Anyone with an unusual marking or feature? How small a marking would be big enough to join, and would it have to be in a really significant place? Or would it be voluntary, so that anyone who identified with our cause would be free to join? But what was our cause, or was there any cause at all? If there are only two of you in the world, you don't really rise to the level of a minority. We were not a public story, just different enough to matter in a personal sense. It was like being disabled, but compared with those who were really disabled, we were privileged; physically we could do anything, and mentally too, but where the mind *met* the body, there it was a somewhat different matter. Ours was the problem of minor though noticeable difference on the frontier of the visible, where what was inside met the outside world, and the outside world came back in. So would we be a gaudy, cavalier group, a carnival of the spotified and spectacular, making our way down the streets? Or would we simply move along through our lives, looking for recognition of a different kind?

Everything is difference. To say this is not to say much, whether it concerns skin colour or birthmarks or the shape of a nose. But some difference makes a difference. A Dalmatian has spots and feels resplendently itself, while others have spots and can feel slightly better than damned. Many years later a woman in our serene town of Amherst buttonholed me at a social function and asked me the inevitable question. When I gave the usual answer, she said, oh well, she had asked because it looked as if someone had hit me; she couldn't resist the usual additional element. Then, because it is that sort of town, she added, I bet you more men than women ask you that question. I mumbled something, because in our town to deny the inherent violence of men is to risk immediate confirmation as unredeemed, so one is guarded. The truth was that I didn't know who asked me more often until, faced with the question, I thought about it and realised that in my adult life it is women who ask me most of the time, though not all of them are equally intrusive. For many it may be simply because women are more conversational than men about personal things, and don't mind sharing mutual details so much. Men, perhaps because they are aware that intrusion always carries the risk of violence, are more careful of private space, and so for the most part they leave me alone. They really don't want to ask who hit me. For whatever reason, I have come to value the quietness of men in these circumstances, the dignity they have allowed me through silence. But it also means I usually live in the world of the unspoken, of wondering what people think or see.

Many years later in Rome, in a street near Piazza di Santa Maria in Trastevere, I saw a man who had one half of his face completely covered in a dark-brown crusty and globular substance. I barely saw him as he passed in the other direction in the flow of the crowd, so that even now I cannot be sure of what I had seen. In the instant I was filled with complex emotions. There was the instinct to turn away, partly out of pity, partly out of recoil, and yet there was identification, because wasn't this me in a starker, more extreme form? Yet what a relief too that it wasn't me. I was aware of my instinctive complicity, not only with the man but against him: I too had noticed markings on someone else, I too had been subject to pulses of the nervous system that travel faster than thought, responses that went deeper than any conscious inclination or will. What I could never know was how much this was because of my marking or his. I couldn't say, and it was all so quick. Yet there he was, walking the street with a studied kind of challenge and dignity, as I was walking in my own way through the world.

We continued into the piazza to be confronted by a most remarkable scene. On the far side of the square was a banner, and it read '*Non c'è futuro senza memoria*'—'There is no future without memory'. As the sun set and it grew dark, a ceremony was about to take place, a commemoration of 16 October 1943, the day the round-up of Jews by the Nazis began in Rome. Most of the deported were dead within a week, and in the synagogue in Rome we had seen the very few seats marked for the survivors who returned. Now we saw an impressive array of dignitaries, including the president of the region and the president of Niger who must have been visiting and had come to pay his respects. He was tall and charismatic, looking like a dark vivid sculpture in the waning light. There were cameras and sound, and large candles held aloft by people of every description, including a number of Africans in flowing robes. Around the square people held signs aloft bearing the names of the German concentration camps, Sachsenhausen, Dachau, Auschwitz, all the others. The event was sponsored by the Jewish community of Rome and the Church of Sant' Egidio, and there were two brief speeches, one by a priest. Then a solemn march began, following the banner, perhaps the march of the deported. We joined for a while, then left.

Two days later in Florence, we visited the extraordinary synagogue, built in the post-ghetto period of Napoleonic conquest and liberation, and saw there the names of the deported of the city, including one Amelia Gallico, and what seemed to be her parents and whole family. I thought of our own older daughter, Amelia, and what the irreversible fate of selection meant, to be marked out for sacrifice. The synagogue had been used as a garage by the Nazis, its holy ark attacked with bayonets, the marks still visible on the wood, now part of its history, its memory, its future. But what a relief and joy also to see the resplendent and defiant building with its exotic and intricate decorations, its lush paintwork and geometric patterns imitating the East, all carried out in what has been called the emancipated, the emancipated, the oh-so-emancipated style.

26

We called the headmaster of our school 'The Boss', and he was reputed not to wear socks; perhaps they were flesh-coloured and appeared invisible. At a certain point he fell in love with the mother of a boy who lived in our neighbourhood, and left his wife to marry her, which caused something of a scandal. He it was who gave me advice when I was fifteen on how adversity makes you stronger—not bad advice if I had been in a mood to take it, but I was not really in that sort of a mood.

I had been playing in the end-of-year cricket tournament at the Wanderers where all the schools played one another, and the Transvaal provincial team was selected at the end of the week. By all accounts I was a natural selection, not only to be in the team but to captain it, something which almost everyone I spoke to took for granted. Perhaps I took it for granted too. I was then playing in our school first team, and this was but an under-fifteen tournament. But expectations did not match the reality; I had some low scores, and on the one day I batted extremely well, I did so early in the morning before the selectors had time to come around and watch. One of the luminaries was a man with the notable name of Dickie Bird, who came from England and later became an internationally famous umpire. I believe he both umpired and selected during the week, and we were meant to be honoured by his presence, though he may have broken the international sports boycott of South Africa to be there. I had seen eminent visitors before—not only the great soccer player Sir

Stanley Matthews but also the cricketer Sir Len Hutton, who once saw me bat at practice and was highly complimentary. On a regular basis my father would take me to L.F. Palmer's, the sporting store in Commissioner Street, where Johnny Waite worked. He had played wicket-keeper, famously, for South Africa, and I was bold enough to count him as a fan because he was gracious enough to take my seriousness seriously. There he would help me select a bat or try on boots; it was amazing to see and be with these people in an ordinary and down-to-earth way.

But during this week something happened, and I marked it as the beginning of the end, for not only was I not chosen as captain, I was not even selected for the province. Instead of heading off to play in the inter-provincial tournament, I was chosen as a member of the pro-forma 'B' team, which would play no one, and I would now have an empty summer stretching before me. It felt fiercely unjust, and given the nature of how things worked at our school, rightly or wrongly I suspected the worst—trading between coaches, and the usual complications around being Jewish. I remember the burning feeling of waiting for my name to be called and not hearing it, and then the slow walk outside, which was where my headmaster happened to find me and tell me not to worry because the experience would only make me stronger. It was an observation that, given everything in my life, filled me only with a dark and fifteen-year-old contempt.

It got worse after that. Though I had been selected at a very young age for the school first team, I simply could not play for the cricket coach, who was also the History teacher who put his hands down boys' shirts. He subdued my spirit. Where in primary school I had explored my capacities in the most uninhibited and ambitious way, now I felt confined and just could not make things happen. I was wearing glasses—that was a difference—and perhaps had lost my innate spontaneity. But that wasn't the whole explanation. Once, after a run of bad form, I was dropped to the second team. Again I was furious, and spent the day before the match visualising myself batting, practising keeping a ball up in the air by hitting it with the edge of the bat to sharpen my sight and reflexes. Somehow, I had no doubt about what I would do, and the next day, in a game that lasted only one afternoon, I scored a century before the break for tea. So, I was back in the first team, but there the air felt sucked out of me again, and the subdued reality resumed. By my last year of school things had reached the point of no return. The cricket master selected someone else to be captain; he was the master's protégé in the boarding houses and also head prefect. That was how it worked. In primary school my coach had allowed me to captain with full authority and imagination; now the master had the head prefect field near him where he umpired so that he could tell him what to do. It was thoroughly degrading, not only for me but for the captain. In the last term of my final year I dropped cricket altogether and never played again for my school. For that matter, I never played again.

What explains it all? A concatenation of circumstances, to be sure. If I had been stronger I might have withstood the obscure weight of the cricket master's presence in my life or even prevailed against him. There was too the mentally dulling environment of the cricketing sports-world. But there was also a certain depression in my being, and it had to do not only with the school. That summer, when I was fifteen and not selected for the province, I travelled instead with my brother's girlfriend Elaine's parents to Plettenberg Bay, where they camped every year. They took me in their car, towing their caravan behind, and we listened to endless tapes of Nat King Cole on the way. A whole entourage came along by various means. There was my brother and Elaine, and Elaine's brother Adrian and his friends who had just finished their year in the army. Kevin, who lived across the road from us, and whose charm could warm you to the tips of your toes, was also there. On the beach one day he and I saved a friend of Adrian's who had fallen asleep in a dinghy and was beginning to drift out to sea down the coast.

The trip was meant to be a pick-up for me, and in many ways it was, as we swam in the sea and ate copious meals which Elaine's father Bubbles, who had been a cook in the army during the Second World War, prepared three times a day with relish and delight. My father drove down to Plettenberg Bay to bring me home, because I had to be back earlier than the others, and he stayed in a local hotel. There one night, I saw him driving with a woman in his car, and when I confronted him afterwards he said there had been a fire on one of the hills, and all the guests at the hotel had gone out to look; he was merely giving someone a lift. The idea of my father, who never went anywhere, driving out specially to inspect a fire was completely bizarre, and when I saw him again with the same woman, after previous experiences in that department the explanation didn't wash. In the few days remaining I stayed out too long in the broiling sun on the beach, and by the time we left in my father's car the whole of my back was on fire. During the hot and silent drive through the Karoo I came out in blisters, and what remained of my skin came off and stuck to the vinyl of the seat. I was peeled, and raved that night in the hotel where we stopped over. At home it felt as if my flesh was going mute under the skin.

⟿ 27

Back in time, go back in time.

'Hello; hello; hello; hello.' A short pause, and then again, 'Hello; hello; hello; hello.' And then again. And again.

This is quite unusual, because it is my father at the phone. Normally my father won't go anywhere near the telephone in the entrance hall, the only phone in the house. He has 'homo-phono-phobia', a man who will not pick up the phone even if he is the person nearest it as he goes by. Of course there is no answering machine, so the phone will ring and ring until someone else does— even to call him to the phone if it is for him, but it never is. There it is, the big black bakelite telephone with its crosswise receiver above its round dial: 43-2569, that is our number and forever will be. (The boy is secretly in love with numbers and their magic: see how $4+3=7$ and $2+5=7$, while 6 and 9 are sequential multiples of 3, all the good numbers; clearly this telephone number is perfect.) But my father is not part of its circuit. Is it because he feels it is beneath him? Or is it anxiety? Who knows who or what summons will be on the other side, what compromises, what involvements are possible? Best to leave that to others. Although one night, somehow, a rare experience occurs. Perhaps one of us has picked up the phone and called my father, but, for whatever reason, he is on it, talking for more than an hour. It turns out it is someone who had been thinking of suicide, who got a wrong number, and my father talked the person down, eased him or her out of it, prevented a death in the world. We are always proud of that. Or that is what we believe.

This, however, is not that night. It is many other nights, over and over and over again. Usually, we are at supper. The phone rings, and like an absolute bolt my father has risen to answer it. But there is no one there, or so he says. And so we hear, 'Hello; hello; hello; hello.' And then again. And then again. Cold anger rises within the boy. Around the table there is tension, and silent signals from his mother. Disregard, disregard, this will pass. Or, I don't know what to do about it, but don't cause a scene. And so they all sit. The boy wants to rush to the phone, seize it from his father, shout to the person on the other side, get off, get out, why do you think you can do this to us! Betrayal is one thing, but stupidity is something else entirely. Just how lame does his father think they are? For he will return to the table and say, wrong number, just a wrong number, a wrong number was all it was. Why then, Dad, did you go on saying 'Hello, hello' for ten minutes while your woman on the other side murmured whatever enticements she felt like whispering into your intoxicated ear. Have your damn affair, do whatever you want, but don't humiliate us like this. There is the event itself, but also its repercussions, for those around the table feel their own silence, their inability, their weakness in not taking a stand. How his mother takes it he does not know. She has weathered similar things before, but this feels like a particularly decadent and horrible phase.

And other things. His father has taken to coming home from the wrong direction. He wouldn't know this, except that sometimes when he is walking home up Bezuidenhout to De la Rey and then Mons, his father will come driving that way too, though it is the wrong way from town. His father will slow the car, offer him a lift, but he declines; no, says the boy, he is nearly home and prefers to walk. One of his friends tells him, how come we see your father

113

so often in Sandringham, at Mrs C's house—they are good friends of your family, aren't they? He knows very well we don't know Mrs C at all, but my mother does, because at a certain point she telephones Mrs C and threatens to take her for everything she has if things continue as they are. This is after Mrs C has been with my father on a business trip to South West Africa; we have seen the pictures my father took from the plane. My mother has gumption sometimes, and this is one of these occasions, and eventually things draw to a close, but they will never be the same. My father's exploits have coincided with the rush of his business success at his firm; but strangely the end of his affairs comes to mean the end of his business success as well.

The boys have seen other things too. Once, when they were quite small they built a hut out of the bamboo stalks that grew at the bottom of the garden. The plan was to stay there overnight, though in the event it was much too scary. But there is an image that remains of something they saw in the morning from that hut. Their father comes out of the house, walking along the wall, and he is carrying a ladder. This in itself seems almost impossible, for apart from mowing the immaculate lawn with geometric precision every Sunday morning, their father does no work at all on the house. But he takes the ladder, and goes up it to inspect the large light outside his bedroom window. Eyes drift from the scene a bit, because after the initial surprise it is not that interesting. But then something has happened. There is a crash and glass has shattered, and there is his father clutching his hand, his wrist, teetering on the ladder. It is an accident, it must be an accident, and there is hospital, and there my father nearly dies, because they give him penicillin, and he is allergic, and comes close to ending his life. But a wrist, and glass, and blood; it was something he wanted to look like an accident.

How many hidden realms of feeling, pain and suffering were there in my father? He didn't say, and I will never know. He tortured

114

us, he tortured my mother, but was he himself tortured, and by what? With those 'hello, hellos', what was he really listening to, whose echo, whose torment, whose forbidden desire? 'Well, if that's how you feel I'll just go and cut my throat.' We heard that enough times almost to get used to it, though the chill of what it actually meant never left us. And then, after the affairs, after the business exhilaration, there years later is his father in his big brown easy chair, speaking to no one, saying nothing, listening to no radio, reading no books, waiting for the day to disappear so he can open the whisky bottle and have his one glass with ice and soda before going to bed and waking up in depression again the next day.

⌒ 28

When he was small, his mother read to him. He remembers the Noddy books, with Noddy, and Big Ears in his car, and the policeman, and the naughty black Golliwog, all taken for granted as populating the natural universe of these stories. Later, more Enid Blyton, though he reads them himself: the Famous Five, the Secret Seven, the world of mystery and intrigue. There are the boys' annuals, and the Life series called *Knowledge* which in the pre-internet world became an almost poignant compendium of what we knew. The English schoolboy volumes come thick and fast. His favourites are the William books by Richmal Crompton (was the author man or woman, he wondered, but never asked), with William himself at the centre, unkempt, tie and cap askew, always inventing half-baked theories of conspiracy with his friends, annoying his sister's suitors, and getting into every kind of scrape. For some reason, William is always falling into the rhododendrons (how does one pronounce that?—it sounds like rho-*dod*-ende-rons in his mind). Billy Bunter is somewhere in there, the fathead member of the upper fourth, or fifth, or sixth—he can't remember—along with Hurree Jamset Ram Singh. Kim comes along, and the *Thirty Nine Steps*, the full panoply of the colonial curriculum, and another comic hero of the so-very-English boarding school named Jennings. And *Jock of the Bushveld*, the dog we could all love, the runt of the litter with his fierce courage and loyalty, and stirring tales of Bushveld allure.

In flies the intrepid Biggles by Captain W.E. Johns, in his Sopwith Camel alongside Ginger and Algy—or were those William's chums?—moving through the First World War and beyond, in tales of dogfight and desert. The Hardy Boys add their American dash, though their lives seem bland by comparison. His mother is a reader, his aunt has bookcases filled to the brim, and at times he will muse his way along them, imagining another world. He reads *The Longest Journey*, about a solitary escape through the Gobi Desert during the Second World War. He sees, but does not read, Norman Mailer's *The Naked and the Dead*, and the same is true of Nadine Gordimer's *The Lying Days*. Instead it is still adventure stories, though of a graduated kind, that attract him, *Where Eagles Dare* and *Ice Station Zebra* by Alistair MacLean, while his mother reads Maigret instead, talking of their psychological insight. His friend David passes on to him the adventures of Archy and Mehitabel—Archy the cockroach with the transmigrated soul who pumps out poems by jumping nightly on the keys of a typewriter, Mehitabel the cat who has seen better days, and nights. *Whatthehell Archy, toujours gai, toujours gai*. Sometimes there is music. In Bach's Brandenburg Concertos he hears the intricate geometries of the cosmos revolving in stately joy and perfection, and listens to them for days at a time.

John Fowles and Dylan's sad-eyed lady are already in the past when he takes on *The Sound and the Fury*, and certain lights begin to go on: oh, different voices are telling the story, and one of them is a backward child, and that is how it works, and I can put it together, I really can. And then there is the moment at sixteen or seventeen when, on his mother's recommendation, he sceptically tries *The Tin Drum* and is captured completely. 'Granted: I am the inmate of a mental hospital', which Günter Grass will later say is the sentence that opened everything. And that grandmother hiding Oskar's grandfather under her voluminous four skirts in the Kashubian potato field where his mother is conceived. And Oskar's deviant drum and Danzig and the rostrum and *there was once a musician ...*

This was another world entirely, this was another way to tell it, this was the book that had been waiting for *him* so that nothing would ever be quite the same.

At high school he makes his way, still withdrawn and abstracted, mind on hold, waiting for something without knowing what. Early on he suffers ostracism of a kind when one of the boys seems to invent a word game targeted at him so that whenever he appears, particular words come up. *Ecce* is the one that seems to apply to him; *ecce homo*, can this be what they mean, but why? His friends take on nicknames, so that Clive is *Claav* (exaggerated Sutheffrican accent), David *Shtan* and Colin *Bubble*. Roy is a Springbok swimmer and writes out his Latin notes in the minutest hand for study purposes. Tim the Australian has come and gone. His best friend is still Barry who, like him, is teaching himself the guitar, working up 'Alice's Restaurant', which he eventually gets with amazing accuracy. From time to time there are talent competitions. He is not a natural performer, but plays with a boy called Terry or with Colin. Sometimes they go on trips to provide music for the aged or disprivileged. What did the aged and disprivileged make of their versions of Simon and Garfunkel, Cat Stevens or Jethro Tull? Hadn't they suffered enough? Others are more daring. Rory fashions an instrument out of a tea-chest, a stick and a rope, and strums a pounding bass on the rope while slapping his bare foot on the chest and bawling out 'Parchman Farm'. So this is what real art is like—that kind of daring and total commitment of the self. Leonard plays the most beautiful classical music on the oboe, something virtually unheard of in our world, but he has a French surname, so that might explain it. There is a boy named William one year behind us whose father is a prominent anti-apartheid lawyer, who seems to be taking to art, who is tremendous at debating, who as a budding theatre director puts on a bravura version of Ionesco. What will become of him?

The final days of the final year have arrived. We write our matric exams, a long series over three weeks in the school hall under invigilation, identified only by number. After the very last exam, the deputy headmaster sees me in the quadrangle, heading out with my friends. He taught me English in Form Two, and once said I should be a palaeontologist, like Professor Tobias—not a bad idea, if only I had known what a palaeontologist actually did. He has a sense of how disenchanted I have been, and may have said something about it now. I want to talk with you, he says, will you come to my office? I consider the idea for a full three seconds, but the world beyond school already beckons. No, I answer, I have something else to do. Fine, I'll write to you, he says, but the letter never comes, and from time to time in years after I wonder what it would have said.

☞ 29

Seeing here, seeing there, images take shape in the air.

Nine thousand miles and some forty years away, our cat Minky stretches out on the sofa for many hours a day, as her predecessor Clio did before her, and her successor Vuvu will do later. She sleeps much of the time, especially in the heat and humidity; in winter it is the warmth of the house she folds into. Now, in summer, she loves the evenings and nights and early mornings, when she goes outside onto the hill planted with rocks and trees and bushes, which in memory of another place we have called, to ourselves, Bosbokrand. We can imagine buck there, but mostly silhouettes against the African dawn and dusk. Early in the summer we have peepers, and later the cicadas, a rhythmic pattern of sound rising and falling, reminding us of our elsewhere. Minky loves the stones, inspects her territory, and especially on moonlit nights invites us out. We walk at night, Minky attending us, sometimes ahead, sometimes behind, sometimes off to the side as she investigates an item of interest. She is happy, clearly proud to be our escort, tail up behind her like a beacon, showing us around in her medium, the dark and flowing currents of the night.

Sometimes on the sofa or our bed she will gaze up. Her cat eyes, narrow, then ease, mysterious yet there, making contact. She will open up, curl over, arm over her eyes, offer her chest and belly, and invite the tickling and stroking and soft murmurs she knows will follow. Minky was a foundling, like Clio before her. Clio would keep me company while I wrote, a soft weight on my lap, or walk across the desk and sit on the windowsill, looking out into the garden. Both found us, or we found them. Now Minky lies on the bed or sofa and gazes up, and her gaze intrigues me, invites me, holds me off. When we go away she misses us; when we return it takes her a while to forgive us, to find her former rhythm and trust. She knows that when we are around, strange things happen. Doors open and shut, a water bowl appears (she knows what a bowl is, she just doesn't know the word), it fills with water. She can count to two: when she knows both of us are up she makes a beeline—or catline—for the bedroom, to lie on the bed. In other words, there is much going on there, between her and us, and we have decided to live together to find out what it is.

When I was in school at the age of thirteen or fourteen, a guidance teacher asked us to go away over the weekend and come back with an argument for the existence of God. It wasn't a proper assignment, just a thought of something we might do. As for the guidance teacher, usually such people were gym teachers given duties they (and we) wished they didn't have, but he had been reading something interesting, and so passed it on to us. When we came back on the Monday, he had forgotten all about it, but I had been thinking about it and must have reminded him, and so I had to speak. The best I could manage had nothing to do with logic, 'the greater than which cannot be imagined' or anything like that, nothing to do with the sheer momentousness of Creation. Rather, I said if I had to fashion an argument it would be based on the idea that humans and animals can understand each other, can communicate across whatever barriers there are between them. Something flowed between us, I said, and that was equivalent to what we might, if we wanted to, call God.

When Minky looks at us, she will sometimes stretch out a leg, reaching for something she wants to touch, stretching towards us for connection. She doesn't live with other cats, she lives with us, we have given our lives to one another. Clio's ashes are buried in our garden. Perhaps our magic powers of doors and water bowls are godlike powers to her, I don't know. Surely she doesn't think of it that way, though she is not without appreciation for what we do. But what I see in her eyes—cat eyes, much more wild than dog eyes—is a reaching, a gaze, for something right there at the edges of what she is able to feel and see. It feels she is saying something like this: within the limits of my capacities, here I am reaching as far as I can in my connection with you. She has also left us headless mice on the pathway in the morning. But there she is, at the limits of her being, the cat who kills and wants to express her love, together.

She does it simply. She lives with nothing, no possessions, no thing she can call her own. Yet she will live her life in this house. We have all kinds of things, including the house, though we don't own the cat and would never claim to. What, though, I sometimes want to know, is on the edge of our being, just beyond our gaze, who is opening doors for us, bringing us water bowls? How would we feel towards such a being, if there were one? What of those things we cannot see, dark energy or matter, folded dimensions or parallel membranes we cannot probe? Do we also reach, stretching out, trying our hardest in moments we are not conscious of doing so, most ourselves when we are unaware? There it is, just beyond our limits, and for the life of us we just cannot get there. Here, across the distance and time of Bosbokrand under the moon in the currents of the night, sometimes that is what we feel.

Mirror World

30 ⌒

Please God, let me go blind.

I am sitting out on a hill, in the blinding sun, drab brown hat on my head, drab brown boots on my feet, drab brown uniform on my body, gleaming rifle in my hand. We have been on an exercise—shooting range, drills in the veld, who knows what—and now there is a short break. Overhead a distant plane is in the sky, a Boeing on its way somewhere, faint trails behind it. And I have reached the point where I am asking God to make me go blind so I can get out of the army. God does not agree to the request, though sometimes in later years I wonder if he may have heard part of it, as my left eye gets progressively worse.

Things did not start well, and how could they? First there was the dreaded moment when we had to register for military duty. South Africa had been in an incipient state of civil war for some time, and there were threats on the borders. All white males were subject to call-up; in recent memory it was a selective, random affair, so you could get lucky and miss it altogether. Now everyone had to go, and they had extended the term of duty from nine months to a year. Or, there was a choice: nine months with compulsory short camps afterwards for a number of years, or twelve months with no further obligation. I opted for twelve. No one was there to tell me I didn't have to go, that there were alternatives, for they were very few indeed, and the idea of outright opposition seemed all but unthinkable. The choices were to leave the country, quite possibly forever, or refuse to serve and be sentenced to military detention—much worse than civilian jail. And then be called up again, and again, ad infinitum. Some would leave—Anthony from down the road did so, heading first to Yugoslavia, where his family came from, but Yugoslavia would have nothing to do with white South Africans, even those fleeing military service in an unjust regime, and eventually he ended up in Holland. A few years later a movement of conscientious objectors and draft resisters emerged, and channels opened up in England and elsewhere; but not now, not for me. My brother had preceded me—went to the Air Force in Pretoria, did his time and came out—and it looked as if I would have to do the same. So, I registered and got my number: 70517152, or at least that's what I remember now. I applied for the Air Force or Navy, but eventually received my papers for the Services Corps in the Army. The very name of it was obscure to me. What or whom did the Services Corps serve, apart from the servitude of serving? As it was, it did not protect me from the regular brutalities of the army, at least not during basic training.

And so there I was sitting on a hill hoping to go blind. On that first day, my parents had taken me to Milner Park, butterflies in my stomach, no sleep the night before. I resolved to be brave, wanted to be brave, but I was only seventeen, how young for this. A crowd milled around in the morning, army trucks lined up like vultures surveying their prospects. We were formed up somehow, and then in my group a corporal arrived to say, who are the cricket players?—we want the cricket players. It was almost a joke: I had heard about not volunteering for anything in the army, and yet I also knew that sportsmen got privileges. What should I do? I have my cricket bag, take a breath, and step forward. All of us who do so are loaded onto a truck, and then the corporal comes, beats the rear of the truck with his hand, and shouts, Congratulations, *roofies*, you are going to Lens! 'What the fuck!' is the simple rendition of what goes through

126

the mind of virtually everyone there, and we all start heading to the back of the truck to escape, but no such luck. We are meant to go to Pretoria, a relatively soft option, but Lens is Lenasia, one of the more godforsaken camps on earth. *Ja*, says the Corporal with a gleeful smile on his face, there were too many for Pretoria, and we need cricket players at Lens. Congratulations, *roofies*, he says again, using the Afrikaans word for new conscripts, for we are the lowest of the low. He shuts the back with the clang of eternity, and we take off at speed. It is a '*roof*-ride' to Lens, the driver alternately accelerating and slamming on the brakes, so that we go sliding and colliding on the benches in the back, all to rattle us, shake us, reduce us to wrecks before we get started.

At the camp we piled out, formed lines in the sun. How desolate it all looked, a bare earthen parade ground, low-slung grey barracks like a factory for churning out mutant soldier-people. Each of us is given a canteen for water, and a dixie for food, still thick with grease from the previous *troepie*'s last meal. And then a haircut, the inevitable haircut for these long-haired hippies from Jo'burg—*what you think, you think this is Hillbrow where you can just go looking for poes!*—and it doesn't matter what you request of the person with the grandiose title of barber, it will all be shaved off just the same. No name, a number, no hair, and then more lines for what is generously called a 'medical'. Here it is underpants down while someone checks hands and teeth and grabs you by the testicles—*hande, tande, hoes!* (hands, teeth, cough!, to test for tuberculosis, perfect assonance and alliteration in the guttural but often amusing Afrikaans)—and there is a blood pressure test as well. And suddenly, I am different, because my blood pressure is high, too high. Maybe I will be rejected, or at least get a G4 rating so I can get a desk job. The medic speaks to me, almost kindly: Go and rest for a bit, and we will call you again. He tells me to sit in the shade, to help my pressure go down, but instead I sit in the sun and think desperately of every last abysmal thing I can to help my pressure go up. But when I am called back, it is down. I am in the army, G1, nothing I can do about it.

That night, terror strikes. At three o'clock there is pounding on the metal doors of the barracks with rifles, and the corporals come rampaging through to wake us up. We have to make our beds for inspection, be ready for anything at any moment. Some who claim to know the drill have already made their beds the night before and then slept on the floor so as not to crease anything. But now we wait, and wait, and wait, and nothing happens until dawn. We sit next to our beds in silence and wait, and in the near distance is the sound of a train going somewhere, away from here, the most melancholy sound I have ever heard. A radio clicks on, and Nilsson is singing plaintively, 'I can't live if living is without you'. I don't even have someone to live without. I feel the comedy but also the abjection. It is an extremely lonely and very sorry feeling.

31

Early in the first week they are lined up on the parade ground when some names are called out, including his. He goes forward to join the small group, and then hears the news: his school has nominated him to go on an officers' training course. An officers' training course: what calamity is this! Is this their final revenge? The school that resolutely kept him a private at cadets, that refused him other recognitions, now wants him to serve the South African regime as an officer? Isn't it bad enough simply being in the army? The hell with that, he thinks, and his first formulation of freedom in the army takes shape. They have my body, they can force me to be here, but they will never have my mind, I will not be an officer, not under any conditions. I will not be a willing participant in my own subjugation or that of others.

In due course he tells them of his resolve, and gets a screaming response. Does he know what he is doing? Is he aware of what happens to people like him? He will be posted to the border, to Grasfontein, truly a hellhole, for secret operations in Namibia, goodbye to the Services Corps, it is the infantry for him, they will transfer him. But he does not give in, and there is another trick up his sleeve, the first of many. He has been selected to go on an exchange programme overseas, to a high school in the United States, and will be leaving for a year in June, to complete his army service afterwards—a rare but regular practice. Therefore he cannot go into the infantry, he needs to stay near Johannesburg or

129

Pretoria so he can study to prepare for his departure. He conscripts his parents to participate in this enterprise: letters are written to commanding officers, things pointed out. In fact much of this is complete fabrication: he does not need to study, and perhaps should be ashamed of his duplicity. Is this not a contradiction of his principles? But other genes have kicked in, and they are the genes of survival, the kind that got his ancestors through a few centuries in Russia. You do what it takes; they can imprison you, but you don't have to cooperate; this too is what resistance can look like. And so, miraculously, early on he is transferred to Pretoria, where he should have been in the first place. That is how it works.

In Pretoria basic training begins in earnest. Under the martinet commands of the drill sergeant there are endless and punishing manoeuvres on the scorching sand of the parade ground (smoke break the only relief at routine intervals), and they go off into the veld as well where they learn leopard crawls and other techniques of their craft. There are also bizarre exercises, a bit like war games, where everyone gets lost and the real aim is to hide out for a while where no one can find you so you can go to sleep—the primary and perpetual imperative in the army. On one occasion out there it pours with rain and the tents are flooded, everything thick with wretched mud. They are in sleeping bags on the ground, and he sees socks floating by. The most crucial thing you own—and they beat this into your head—is your rifle, and whatever you do don't ever, ever, *ever* call it a gun. (There is a rhyme to that effect: *This is your rifle, this* (pointing to the crotch) *is your gun; this is for shooting, this is for fun.*) So the rifle is tucked up in the sleeping bag as well: you can drown, but keep your rifle dry. And there is abuse of various kinds, motifs so common that everyone knows them. *Sien jy daardie boom?* (Do you see that tree?—pointing vaguely to a clutch of trees in the distance.) *Sien jy daardie blaar?* (Do you see that leaf?) Well, go fetch it for me, now, NOW! *HARDLOOP, jong, HARDLOOP!* (Run,

130

boy, run!) You run to the trees, fetch a leaf, bring it back. *Nee, man, nie* daardie *boom nie!* (Not *that* tree.) *HARDLOOP WEER!* (Run again!) Come back with another leaf, to find it was the right tree but the wrong leaf, so you have to run again.

People are threatened, the corporal's crooked teeth are in your face, someone gets hit. Once at the shooting range, a poor *roofie* puts up his hand because his rifle is stuck and he needs help. Drill sergeant comes over; *roofie* makes the mistake of pointing the rifle at him to explain. *Roofie* gets kicked, nearly to death. Phrases get repeated, lines they begin to know like the refrain of a tired song. From the short lieutenant, who did go on the officers' course: *Ek's klein maar ek is 'n trein* (I'm small but I'm a train—inference, don't mess with me). From the ugly bugger corporal with the crooked teeth: *Wat smile jy, dink jy ek is 'n hoer?* (What are you smiling at, do you think I'm a whore?) Push-ups in the morning, star-jumps for punishment, holding your arms out interminably to the side for meaningless torture.

He makes friends there, Barney and Alan, Jewish boys, and how intense and quick the friendships are, just someone to talk with, compare notes. Towards the end of basic, Barney and Alan hear they will indeed be transferred to the infantry, standing guard at a notorious camp in Kimberley, and they begin to withdraw from him just a bit. Still, there are at least two intriguing developments at this time. One is, he is well on his way to becoming an inveterate liar, something that will only deepen during his period in the army. For always you have to be thinking: not only what is the answer, but what answer are they *expecting*; and not only what answer are they expecting, but how can I subtend a hypotenuse from *that* to a line that will keep me safe? Most importantly, how can I get out of it—whatever *it* happens to be? And you have to do it at speed, right in the moment, complex negotiations and calculations. By the time his twelve months are up he is convinced that if some stray person in the street were to ask him the time, just by reflex the mental gears would whirr into action as he worked out what answer to give—and it would probably be the wrong one. There is genuine concern that he may never be able to tell the truth again.

The second thing is that he is surrounded in the army mostly by dyed-in-the-wool Afrikaner nationalists, both instinctive and conscious supporters of apartheid, and sometimes there is heated argument about this, though you have to be careful. But in his platoon by the end of basic training, all of them, whether nationalist, liberal or whatever, have come to an implicit agreement on one point. If war was ever to break out, and should those bas-tards make the mistake of giving us actual bullets to put in our rifles (the principal rule in our experience is that they never trust us with live ammunition), the first ones to go will be them. First will be the ugly-bugger corporal with crooked teeth, then the drill sergeant, then the lieutenant who is a *trein*, and no one will ever know. Fortunately, war never breaks out.

32 ⤺

Basic training is over, and I have been assigned to Doornkop, also known as Diepkloof, where Alan Paton once served as head of a reformatory, a fitting echo of a kind, but that is not on my mind right now. The camp is over the road from Soweto, first flashpoint in any coming crisis, though the South African state will be in serious disarray if it has to rely on conscripts like us for its defence. We live in tents. I have my *trommel* (metal chest at the bottom of my bed), my *kas* (metal wardrobe, though that is a glorified term), and my bed-card, listing name, rank and serial number. This is who I am. My job is to be storeman (what the Services Corps, among other things, does), working in a converted aircraft hangar which houses everything from bed-frames and mattresses stacked high towards the roof, to socks, underwear, shoelaces, belts, boots, rocket-propelled grenade launchers, R1 rifles modelled on the Belgian FN, and submachine-guns modelled on the Israeli Uzi. It is an all-purpose store.

My companions are Louis (dark-haired, unguinous) and Piet (blond, lively) who have been there for some time and are therefore owed all kinds of deference. There are also *roofs* like myself—Peter (Anglo, from Springs or Benoni) and Michael (Greek, also called Michallie, with the guttural Greek 'ch' sound). And I am Jewish; at least we cover the various permutations. Peter is dry, reserved, intelligent; Michallie is intelligent and wild. He it is who comes out with the frequently obscene deprecations ('If the captain was on fire I wouldn't cross the street to piss on him') or teaches us extremely

133

basic Greek for use with girls ('I want to fuck you'). Piet and Louis are Afrikaners, and their phraseology is different, but oriented towards the same ends. Thus, Piet, after a weekend pass and an encounter with some females, slapping his fist on his hand and using a rudimentary petrol-station analogy: *'Pomp en maak vol, ek sê!'* ('Pump, and fill it up, I tell you.') Like everything else in the army, all tends towards the fundamentals, and usually in the crudest of terms.

What do we learn? For one thing, our extended training in the ways of deviousness is sustained. I am assigned to the armaments section of the store, where I work with Louis under a sergeant. Here, wearing light khaki overalls for daily use, our primary objective is not to be seen. There are inviting hideaways behind storage bins and shelves, and if you work it right you can always sneak ten minutes or so to go to sleep. It is not that we are short of sleep: there is no electricity in the tents and the nights are long, but boredom and anxiety bring their own promptings, and so sleep is a premium, almost a currency, a highly prized way to be unconscious through it all. Sleeping on the job is its own kind of minor triumph. Sometimes we are called out to help in other parts of the store, and there one day I manage to fall asleep while pushing a trolley—no mean achievement, and afterwards I am rather proud. There are other forms of resistance. If an order comes in for bed-frames, we have to climb to the top of the high piles to get them, sometimes twenty or thirty feet in the air. How to get them down? Simple: *throw* them down, right from the top. Springs, rivets and bolts go scattering away, but that is not our problem. The problem belongs to the sad *moegoes* on the other side who will sign for the frames without checking them. We are destroying enemy property; it's just that the enemy is our own army.

The enemy are also the PFs—permanent force members who required no conscription to account for their present circumstances. In other words, they signed up voluntarily. By and large these are

134

Afrikaners, under-educated, finding protected employment in an all-white army that guarantees them jobs and even promotion. No PF but he is at the very least a corporal, and usually a sergeant, sergeant-major, lieutenant or captain. These people steal the army blind, their own kind of war effort but with a different purpose. I have seen it in the canteen. Whereas we *troepies* are given porridge with maggots to eat, and meat that seems to require something still to make it die, all the best cuts find their way to the homes of the PFs. In the store it is exactly the same, and there is nothing like the amount of goods housed there that there ought to be.

One day the military police arrive at the store, towards closing, and round up the conscripts. They are targeting theft, and we have been identified as the problem. We form up into a small platoon, and the MPs quick-march us towards the tents, where they make us halt some distance away. We are to remain there under guard, while each of us is taken in turn to our tent, where we must unlock our *trommel* and *kas* to be searched. Though I have stolen nothing, in the army there is always incipient fear. Something will go wrong, maybe they will plant something, maybe in a narcoleptic state I took something from the store without knowing, maybe the laws of physics have been suspended and something will simply be *there*. For Michallie it is even more acute. He has not stolen anything, but he has brought in some bottles of alcohol, at present residing in his *trommel*. If caught, he will go to DB—detention barracks—where he can expect only the worst. Michallie stands there in silent terror and squirms, not knowing what to do.

We get called off, one by one. Peter is marched away to our tent, and he must be OK, because in a while he returns, standing a little way off, now free to come and go. Michallie makes his way to the edge of the group and manages to throw his keys to Peter while the guard is turned away. Then I get marched off, heart beating, not knowing what to expect, but when I open my *kas* and *trommel* for

135

the MP they are indeed clean, and I too am free to leave. I haven't seen Peter, but when I get back outside I see that he is again near the edge of the group, and Michallie is being called, and at the last minute Peter throws him his keys, which Michallie picks off the grass, pretending to have dropped them. He doesn't know what has happened, whether Peter was able to get into the tent, so he is marched in, opens his *trommel* and then faints, hitting the ground. His *trommel* is empty, clean. Somehow Peter had done it, moving the alcohol to his own *trommel* and locking it up safely. Michallie staggers out a few minutes later, quaking with relief, while Peter stands there nonchalantly, with perfect aplomb. We have beaten the army once again.

33

Periodically in the store he works as a co-driver, delivering goods to other camps, usually in Pretoria, in the Bedford trucks South Africa has imported from its sometimes detractor, sometimes patron, England. Technically he is there to help navigate, protect the goods, help unload them, be back-up, but basically this is a cushy opportunity to get out into the world again, see the tempting realities of civvy life, and he takes full advantage. One of the drivers he accompanies is also Jewish, and his family owns a celebrated kosher meat-and-sausage emporium in Johannesburg, so they fake their route to go through the city and stop off to pick up polony. He doesn't even like polony that much, but, as with everything else, it is a kind of statement, an embellishment of one's daily existence to hazard the extravagant and fundamentally unnecessary gesture.

Ostensibly the truck's mileage is there for the checking, but no one ever does, so we get more daring. We go through my suburb and stop off at the house, a massive Bedford truck parked at the top of our driveway in Mons Road. Once I even take my laundry home. Michallie, now also a driver, gets into a fury at the army one day while the truck is stopped at a traffic light and kicks the windscreen, leaving a huge crack in the glass. We need to do something to explain it, and Michallie manufactures a plausible version: he had to slam on the brakes suddenly, and cracked his head on the windscreen. On one occasion, nearing Pretoria on the highway, there is the sound of an explosion, and smoke everywhere. When it clears

we are still travelling, careering down the road, and it is evident
something in the truck has blown up. We manage to pull over, but
there are no phones, nothing, so we do what any self-respecting
troepies in the army would—we lie down in the grass and go to
sleep. That is, we do so until an officer passing by on the highway
stops and finds us, and threatens us lividly with DB for dereliction
of duty. On other trips to Pretoria we pass by Pretoria Local prison,
where my father's cousin Baruch is incarcerated for his opposition to
apartheid—the sabotage he had undertaken, blowing up electricity
pylons. His son Denis is just a bit older than I am. I eye the prison
gate awkwardly, aware with an unsettling sense of culpability of the
very different roles being played at that moment by two members
of the same extended family, on either side of the wall. Am I in the
army Baruch's prison-keeper? What would he say?

At other times I feel that being in the army is the closest I will
come to being black in South Africa. That is what it feels like, all
the constrictions, very few rights, the constant madness and abuse.
But there are also blacks in the army—not soldiers, at least not
at this stage—but workers in the store like us, except, as usual,
the blacks are treated worse. Like us, they wear overalls, but of a
different colour: distinction must be maintained. There is meant
to be no contact between us, but every now and again there is,
as we pass someone a sandwich or a cigarette. I ponder how and
why, in this regime, anyone black would end up in the army, but
the answer is simple and self-evident. It is a job, people need food
and money, pitiable as it might be. But the black workers regard
us too with suspicion, and why shouldn't they? To them we are
young whites, privileged by our colour, who represent the apartheid
regime and appear to be doing so willingly. So, there is silence and
a kind of quiet dignity among these black workers: they will not
simply take hand-outs. I can see them now: one rather large, stately,
patrician, others more thin and wiry, moving about the hangar and

its environs, a community of their own. Always there is the intense self-consciousness of the South African condition for someone such as myself. Where do I fit in, just what are the compromises I have made, the exact contours of my complicity? These are questions which with any degree of honesty I cannot ignore.

Just once it all seems to become quite real. We are called out to the training ground at Doornkop, where some Bedfords are lined up; we have our rifles and combat gear. It is 1972: no Soweto Uprising yet, Black Consciousness still in its early stages, no outright war on the border, though there are tales of military action in Namibia and Rhodesia—South African soldiers fighting in Rhodesian uniforms. But someone has decreed it: we are to be trained for urban containment, how to go into a township and put down a rebellion or unrest. So we must pile into the Bedfords and learn how to leap and fan out when they stop. There is a feeling of revulsion inside me, rising into my mouth. Can I do this, will I do it, will I actually get on that truck? And what will I do if the real thing ever comes to pass? Will I participate, will I fire a gun, will I shoot someone? All this flashes through in the lightning-fast form of internal calculation which is now second nature. I don't remember exactly what hap-pened that day. It was some vapid drill, somebody's big idea, we were told about the trucks but never got on, and the Bedfords never came again. But somewhere inside me was the thought: if the real thing ever happens, I will not do it, I will not shoot and will just have to deal with the consequences.

The standard routine takes over, the daily grind, the thick slabs of bread and butter at eleven with tea, the cold inside the hangar as winter approaches, the bitter nights in the tents, so that the fire-buckets, outside, are frozen solid in the mornings. You wear everything you have to sleep: longjohns, tracksuit, pyjamas, greatcoat, and balaclava on your head, waking up dazed in the mornings. Going AWOL becomes a way of life. Passes are few and far between, so one sneaks out on the weekend, getting a lift on one of the trucks going into town, and perfecting the art of getting through the gate again on Sunday night when one returns. There is always the danger of a snap raid or inspection, but it is actually not in the interests of the army to know how many of its soldiers are defective, and one can usually wriggle one's way out of that with a suitable explanation. Sometimes there are real passes, a real return home, and few feelings more dismal than the drive back to camp with my father at ten o'clock on a Sunday night to enter the benighted world once again.

But as usual, absurdity also livens our existence. We have a new captain in the store, and, as with everything else in the army, he has had to sign for it. This is not just one rifle or a pair of boots, your responsibility until the day you *klaar out* and return them. He has signed for the whole store, every last item in it, and he'll have to pay for the difference should anything go missing. Only belatedly it occurs to him that he should have counted everything before he signed; yes, on reflection that would have been wiser. Accordingly, he makes us count. He cancels all passes, we work after hours and on weekends while we count—every last shoelace, every bullet, every pair of underpants, every bed, every mattress, every glove. And of course we come up short, because so much has been stolen. We feel triumphant: that captain is in it now! He will have to pay! But the captain is not a captain for nothing, and he makes us count again. Again, we come up short, in every category every time. So he makes us count again, we are now weeks into this, and we are not conscripts for nothing, so we also get the idea, though admittedly we have been a bit slow. We count, but when the time comes to call out the results, and the captain says, 'johns, pairs of, long', we ask, 'Captain, how many should there be?' He tells us, and miraculously that is exactly the number we have counted. It is the same in every category, the store has everything it should, and the Captain's signature stands good for it all.

140

34 🙟

When I was small, at Clara Patley nursery school in Yeoville, I would sometimes go AWOL, sneaking over the road and across the corner to the block of flats where my uncle Michael and aunt Ethel lived. I must have loved being there, for they were closer in age to me than my parents and seemed free-spirited. Years afterwards Ethel told me that she liked it too—her little visitor. Michael was the youngest of my father's siblings, and much cherished and coddled by his mother, though he had been wild as a youngster. When he was fifteen, he and a friend absconded with a car and went missing, so my father and his brother Stanley had to leave at short notice to drive down to Durban and find him. They arrived, discovered Michael on a beach, then turned round and drove straight back with him through the night so that my father could play a hockey match in Johannesburg in the morning.

Uncles and aunts: oblique biology rather than the direct line, and as such they can show you quite a bit. Stanley, so unlike my father— quiet and thoughtful where my father was instinctive and impulsive, yet still in the same gene pool, a variant as it were—had followed his own father into the insurance business. But his heart was always elsewhere. He loved jazz and classical music, and in time became a collector of Africana, particularly maps of Africa and South Africa which came to line his walls. Later he and his wife Valerie left for London, where they started an insurance business. But Stanley was perhaps the only insurance agent in London who listened to jazz playing behind him on a tape machine in his office through the day. After he retired, he built himself a music room in his house and for the first time in his life took lessons, learning to play classical and jazz pieces on the piano. His music books were on the shelves, black-and-white photos of the jazz masters adorned the walls. He had never been to university, but at last, in his eighties, became a teacher himself, fashioning courses on jazz for the University of the Third Age in London. He compiled his own curriculum for me, sending compilations of the greats, all the way from Louis Armstrong's 'West End Blues' to Art Tatum, Jimmy Rushing and Ruby Braff. Each of us finds our own guides, and Stanley on my father's side was counterpart to Sheila on my mother's. Sheila with her enigma and mystery, Stanley with his music and gentleness: they gestured towards a way along that path over there, as if they were beckoning and pointing at the same time.

As for Michael, he and Ethel were married very young, when he was nineteen and she seventeen. It was something of a scandal, because she was still at school and pregnant, and everything had to be hurriedly arranged. After their son Alan was born they moved from their flat into my grandparents' house, in Eckstein Street. Eckstein Street ran parallel to Mons, though the house was some way away. Soon after they moved, there was drama involving our fox terrier, Laddie—the dog my grandfather had brought. Laddie too would go AWOL, by and large at night, roaming the neighbourhood as dogs did then, and somehow he discovered his way to the house in Eckstein Street, where he would stop outside and howl, waking the baby. We knew about it from Michael's furious response, but instead of phoning us in the middle of the night, it just seemed easier to put the damn dog in the car and bring him home. What we'd hear, at three o'clock in the morning, was the car screeching to a halt in the road outside, and the door slam as Michael chucked the dog out. No wonder Laddie kept going back for more.

142

Michael and Ethel stuck together; they cleaved—it is the only word for it. They had perpetual ups and downs as they tried one venture after another. Usually these didn't go too well, and there would be hushed conversations between my father and Michael at our house. But Mike and Eth always kept going, bouncing up from every disaster to try something new. Early on I loved going to their house; Alan was an amazingly sweet baby, there was the mystery—finally—of a cousin younger than I was, and always an indefinable spirit in the air. As time went on, Mike and Eth tried printing, they opened a restaurant, they did everything under the sun. There was some ambiguity, at least as far as we were concerned, for Michael joined the police reserve, and may have been a Nationalist at heart, at least for a while. Michael loved cars, he loved racing, he loved gadgets, he was the very emblem of what my Granny Ree would have called a *vilde khaye*—a wild animal.

Finally, they struck it rich, for Michael and Ethel started a flag business. At first they made flags for the regime, which needed lots of them, but with eminent flexibility—this took off just as South Africa was changing—they made themselves available to all. The crucial moment was when the new South African flag arrived after 1994, because everyone now needed flags, and Mike and Eth could provide. They had a factory near Alexandra township, and they turned the things out. Always they worked together, every day. They travelled to overseas conferences on flags, they became known internationally. At home they had union troubles in the factory, because these were militant times, and they combined a business-like pragmatism with a real concern for their workers, so that when someone was ill or there was a death in the family, the worker would be taken care of. In later years Ethel, who could tell a story like no one else, would deliver lengthy and hilarious monologues about these events. Cigarette dangling out of her mouth she would declaim, 'They call Winnie Mandela "Mama Afrika". Let me tell you, *I'm*

143

Mama Afrika!' And in a way she was. Every afternoon, at four, vast flocks of birds would come to the house where Ethel, cigarette still dangling, fed them with bread and voluminous sacks of seeds as well as fruit she had cut up for the loeries. Pigeons wandered into their house, but they didn't mind. Even their old dog would lie there with a curious interest but no more.

Once, in a street in New Orleans, where I was talking to someone, I heard a familiar voice, but it seemed unbelievable until I looked up and saw. There was Eth, tugging Michael by the shoulder, saying in her inimitable accent, 'Look, Mike, I told you, it *is* Stephen!' It was the kind of moment that tells you there is more going on than you think. They were part of my earliest life, a continuing rhythm and pulse, and so when in November 2010 Ethel suddenly went into hospital and died, it was hard to imagine how Mike would survive without her, because they were so completely inseparable. It was as if a wave had fallen on the shore, the water had seeped into the sand, and the tide lacked the energy to keep going.

35

In June the time came for me to leave the army for a year and travel
to the United States on exchange. Like everyone else, I had wanted
to go to California or New York City, but instead I was heading
to, of all places, Nebraska, which was a bit like being exiled to a
remote region of the Orange Free State. Still, that was where I had
been assigned, and so I would go. Emerging out of uniform, hair
still insufferably short, I went into orientation with other members
of the programme (easy to make out the army evacuees among us).
We learned about the US, we went down a gold mine to tap into
authentic South African experience, we learned not to say 'rubber' in
America when asking for an eraser, and to alter the words of Jeremy
Taylor's iconic song 'Ag Pleez Deddy' so that we didn't sing about
how we missed 'nigger balls and liquorice' in the chorus but rather
'sugar balls and liquorice'. Then we got on a charter plane for the
trip up Africa, landing in Ghana to pick up other students. What an
amazing feeling that was: not only my first major journey out of the
country, but landing in Africa as well, which would otherwise have
been impossible. Africa seemed an alien and mysterious continent,
not really where we lived. And then on to New York, where we
landed after something like a twenty-one-hour flight. There, in an
almost hallucinatory daze, it was onto a bus in the midnight along
highways to our staging post on Long Island. I still remember the
feel of height above the cars in the coach, the rush of perilous speed,
the lurching and merging and acceleration, the orange haze of lights,

the size of everything, the sense of imminent collision. It was hot summer, and when we arrived the trees were dripping with humidity in the dark.

A day or two in Long Island, and then it was onto another bus, a Greyhound, for the drive across country. New York, Pennsylvania, Ohio, to Indiana (scenes of classic American barns), Illinois and Iowa, dropping off people along the way. Finally we came to Nebraska, last stop, where we reached Omaha at about one in the morning. There I met my host family, and we drove to Fremont some thirty miles away, where Bob—the father—said, 'You might as well get used to this,' and took off his hair. Nothing made visual sense, all was an exaggerated dream, for Bob wore a toupee and didn't want me to be surprised later on. But I didn't know where I was, and fell into the deepest of sleeps.

What did he learn, this venturer from a kind of Africa, in the heartland of what was called America? First, I was fortunate to be placed with a kind and generous family who did their best to understand me and make me comfortable (they were also hosting another boy whose parents had separated and needed stability for the year while he finished school). This family, like mine, was Jewish, though of a rather minimalist kind, and they too had a migrant history, from Eastern Europe to the US, and then on the trains to Nebraska where a clothing store now formed the hub of their lives. Bob had left for a while to be a student at Berkeley, and always felt he might have gone on to other things, but had been called back to run the store and did so, making a wistful peace with reality. He loved ideas, and had a sly sense of humour: 'Come in and save,' he would say wryly of the department store ads. He also told me, as I started shivering into the Fall, that it wasn't cold yet, that it wouldn't be cold until he, Bob, told me it was cold. But they lived in their own world as well. There was Johnny Carson on TV, and M*A*S*H, and All in the Family, and there was golf, endless golf, and the country

146

club where you ordered steak, which drove me mad. The visitor who had come to them was from a police state, he had just been in the army, albeit a bizarre version of one, and here he was, in an insulating chamber of some kind which on occasion could feel quite airless. Thank goodness this family was patient, for he was not the easiest of guests, and he tried to be patient too, for the most part.

Early that summer they gave me a job in the store, to work in exchange for clothes, for under the terms of the scholarship no money was allowed to change hands. Suddenly I was meant to be an expert on clothing and fit, and whether to wash jeans in warm water or cold. But I was less and less interested in things and appearance, and was not exactly a whiz of a salesman; mostly the others in the store looked on me with a genial tolerance. Debbie, who was the perky manager of the downstairs section, invited me home one day to see her gerbil. I had no idea what a gerbil was, and in the South African way didn't ask, because she said it as if I was expected to know; I was mildly disappointed when I got there to see a kind of hamster on a treadmill in a cage. At Debbie's I met her boyfriend David, recently returned from naval service in Vietnam, for that was still under way, a real army in a real war, with real trauma all round. But where the rest of America was in revolt, Nebraska was sedate and conservative. There were no draft dodgers here, no demonstrations, just a kind of mute support for the way things were.

Early on after I arrived I was invited to play music with some neighbours in the fourth of July parade; they were brothers, quite professional, and had built their own studio at home. When I arrived on the appointed day with my guitar, I saw that the float we would be on was decorated in red, white and blue bunting and had a big sign saying 'Re-elect the President'. No way, I told the brothers, there is no way I will set foot on that float. Relax, they told me, no one cares around here, everyone is Republican, and it won't mean a thing to anyone or make any difference. To my shame I was loyal to my musician friends and not my political principles, so we took off, playing 'Mr Bojangles'. Somewhere in the world there is a picture of me playing the guitar in a fourth of July parade on a float supporting Richard Nixon.

But I was the alien there. The head of the local chapter of my programme was a Belgian woman who had made a kind of peace with being in America, but lived with a sense of suppressed frustration. She took me out to lunch and taught me how to listen to the rapid-fire list of salad dressings in a restaurant and choose: Thousand Island, please. I gave talks where Americans would ask me if I knew some people who also came from Africa—they lived in Kenya. Early on I learned the paradox of how people in the most powerful country in the world knew so little about it, while the world knew a great deal about them. 'I've never read those Rooshians,' my English teacher told me when I spoke of Dostoevsky, though she said she wanted to. When the elections actually came around in November, there was a mock ballot in the school. Sitting with the others in my home room, I wrote the name George McGovern on my slip of paper and folded it over carefully. It was meant to be a secret vote, but when the pretty girl collecting the papers came to me, she unfolded mine and announced my choice to the class. There was a small collective gasp, and then a voice speaking for all: 'What does he know, he's just a dumb foreigner!' I was one of three in the room who voted for McGovern.

36

When I first arrived we went out to the river, the Platte. Broad and sunny, it flowed into the Missouri, which fed into the Mississippi, so that you could picture Huck Finn and Tom Sawyer there. That was what it felt like in the warm sunshine, floating down the waters on a large inner-tube taken from one of the farm tractors. I bought OshKosh overalls and cowboy boots, tried these identities on. Carole King wove her tapestry in the clothing store, and on the radio there was other music, 'American Pie' and Carly Simon—the levee was dry and you were so vain, and a horse with no name was making its way across the desert but it was good to be out of the rain. At school I didn't learn much; the history textbook was titled *History of a Free People*, and I knew about history textbooks of that kind. The whole concept of being there was strange, after I had finished school in Johannesburg and been in the army. It required a kind of internal postponement, a numbing.

I met friends, made friends, among them Bobby the minister's son who always had a ready supply of marijuana and smoked it with the most beatific yet concupiscent smile. I tried it too, though you could be sent home in disgrace for that. We were also not allowed to drive, but I couldn't resist the lure of a friend's Mustang in an empty parking lot, using the self-framed excuse that it wasn't a public road—not much good if it came to anything. Once I went across state to visit another school with a boy widely acknowledged to be gay—people imitated his speech, his wrists, but I was secretly curious about his way of being. He was sweet and friendly, but on the way back, in the midst of a rainstorm, he suddenly announced that he could drive no more. So I had to, on the highway, in his car, on the wrong side of the road, with enormous trucks throwing up whole washes of spray, making it impossible to see. One of the South African students on exchange that year was sent home for driving. One of them came home at the end of the year a Jew for Jesus, no doubt a surprise to her parents.

To my own surprise, I became a football player, or to be precise a kicker in the school football team. It happened almost to the classic script. Outside one day, in gym class, in a mood of abstract inquiry I set up a ball and kicked it through the posts. Then I did the same from further away. Then again. A small crowd gathered, not least because I kicked soccer style, a complete oddity around there. The gym teacher alerted the football coach, who told me to come to practice, where I was selected for the team. On average, during our games, I would be on the field for approximately two and a half minutes: my duties included kick-offs, extra points after touchdowns, and field goals. The night of my very first game there was confusion, however. Nervous and excited I put the ball up on the tee for the kick-off and limbered up, pawing the grass from some yards away, waiting for the whistle, raring to go. But why was everyone facing the other way, including my own team, and why were their helmets off? I turned around to see them facing the flag in the breeze while the national anthem lofted across the field. Given my experience, the whole concept of a national anthem, let alone at a school game, seemed a travesty, so I turned around and shuffled my feet in embarrassment. Would anyone notice me if I pretended not to be there?

For the most part in these games it was hard to go wrong, as extra points were virtually impossible to miss, and field goals weren't too difficult—when I got the chance, that is, because my coach

150

seemed to have a moral predisposition against them. There were bad moments, however. Usually, my tasks would take seconds: the extra point is scored and it's all over, or I kick off and someone is tackled, whistle blows and I run off the field. But not always. As a practical matter, I have pulled my face-mask down so that I can see the ball as I run up to kick. On one occasion an opponent puts an elbow in there, nearly taking off my nose. Another time, after I kick off, there is no tackle. The game is going on, someone is running, all is chaos, what should I do? Nobody has told me about this! There is barely time to think when a hulking brute from the other side comes along and flattens me, though I am nowhere near the ball. I get up—and the brute flattens me again. So I lie on the ground until it is all over, army instincts emerging. Then, at the very end of the season, when a field goal will decide not only our final game but the standings in the conference, I am at last sent on by the coach to take a thirty-five-yarder or so. The lines are down, the snap comes back, I am running up, the quarterback places the ball, I kick and it feels perfect, the kind of kick you know will go over as you hit it. But these American balls—they dip and swerve, and a gust at the last second suddenly sees it take a plunge. It hits the crossbar and comes back on the hither side. Two millimetres higher and I would have been a hero. But this is America: tough luck, loser; I go off and the coach will not speak to me, not even to say nice try. But I have a 'letter' to be sown onto my school jacket, and a six-inch statue, a photo of myself as a football player in 1972.

As winter comes, Bob, the father, finally tells me it is cold, and it is, it is freezing, and blizzards blanket the yard. We live indoors at home, and at school, and at basketball games. Yet something in America is turning me away. For underneath it all there is another history, an inner dialogue which no one else knows about, a current I am aware of when everything stops, its flow deep and unavoidable and insistent. I like those girls from Denmark and France on the

151

programme, but what am I really thinking? At some level the sheer thingness of the life around me begins to put me off. America is full of things: there are steaks two inches high, and cars, and weight machines, and muscles, a profusion of matter, an absence of meaning. Ask what someone is like, and the answer is liable to be about six foot two and two hundred pounds. At some level for me there is a profound alienation, it is like South Africa except they don't know it, can't see it, and I find it hard to explain. I retreat into my old familiar domain, silence. I feel the need to rein myself in, make choices. I find a book on existentialism: the word has been on my mind. At the beginning of the year I had put on weight—those school meals with their sloppy joes and sticky cinnamon buns. Now I go more carefully, refusing uninspected wants, choosing every day. My body becomes leaner, thinner, lighter; no one talks about it, but it is there. In June I play tennis down at the courts, hitting the ball for hours on end against the practice wall in the stripping heat, sweating everything out, not eating anything afterwards. It is as if I am answering matter with anti-matter, it is a pursuit of the spirit.

At the end of the school year, a friend and I perform a spoof wearing grass skirts and coconuts. I am never easy performing, but coming back through New York with the other international students, for once I play feral electric guitar at a party while others dance, and a Colombian girl tells me one day I will be famous. Walking through Manhattan on my own I stare at a theatre across an intersection promising what I do not even know how to ask, and besides it is day and everything is closed. What I might have hoped for has been postponed, and when will it come again? I am returning to South Africa, to the army, and who will I be when I get there? The indeterminate boy I really am, or something invented to serve and pretend? One eye looks into the distance, distracted, the other turns inward towards the self.

37

He returned—this he that was I, the I that was he—to South Africa and the army a free man, at least in certain respects, though 'man' was probably the wrong word; he never felt it fully belonged to him, never came to like it. The prospect of the army was of course vile. He had been in the United States, he had grown his hair, he had felt the freedom of water and movement and air. And yet it had been an absent kind of freedom, one that had no bounds, no shape, no contours, no prospects, a state of floating in the winds. Now he has cut his hair—they will certainly cut it for him once he is in—and faces the looming day, a day he cannot later remember. But there has been a change. He has come to a decision, and feels free inside. In his first six months the army beat him, pinched him, wore him down; he was depressed, subjugated, subdued. Now in his new existentialist mode he knows that if he frees his mind, nothing whatever can suppress him. They can do what they want, put him on permanent duty, deprive him of sleep, make him stand guard, cancel every one of his passes. But he has decided to be free. By definition it is a freedom of the spirit; his body will become lighter all through those six months. This is part of his quest, so that he is flying, lifting in another way.

He has reported for duty, but has been reassigned. While his base camp will still be Doornkop, instead of going back to the store he will now be working at the Drill Hall in Johannesburg, the administrative headquarters for the region. It is in many ways the perfect,

153

unimagined assignment. Every day he will be close to the heart of the city, in sight of life, the bustle of people and things passing beyond the walls on the roads and pavements. His specific job is in the records office, and he has been seconded to a sergeant as his immediate boss. The office also houses a sergeant-major, a captain, a major, various PFs, some women staffworkers and other poor *troepies* like him, though he is now no longer a *roof*. The PFs for the most part are the usual: they drink too much, they gamble, they lose money and come asking for loans. Of course they are not allowed to do so; it is strictly against army rules, not to mention a taboo inversion of hierarchy. But the smart *troepies* will always lend them money, even a few rands at a time. Why? Because when you do, the PFs are literally in your pocket, they belong to you. You can always report them, they owe you favours. In short it is a kind of blackmail—the ideal army situation. Beware, however, complacency; those same PFs will betray you at a moment's notice if the opportunity arises. No such thing as loyalty here except the kind that can be bought, rather cheaply at that; what comes easily goes just as fast.

My sergeant, however, is different. He is of Anglo background, not Afrikaner, and his family were SAPs—South African Party before the war, followers of Smuts rather than the nationalist Malan— and that is why he will never be promoted further, though he is, in the scheme of things, comparatively competent at his job. So, my sergeant talks to me, sometimes offers to share his 'sangwiches', as he calls them. But he too asks favours, chiefly to go into the city to buy Oil of Olay for his wife, because he himself cannot bear entering a chemist shop to buy women's things. Though I have never heard of Oil of Olay, I am of course willing to take any opportunity, to be part of real life for an hour, at least in my mind, though what others see, especially the blacks who throng around me on the streets, is another question. There I am, a soldier, a hated soldier in my uniform, boots and blue beret, someone to fear and avoid.

154

Sometimes the small journey is even more fraught, for my sarge runs the Drill Hall bar, and there are often revenues to deposit, so I and another conscript are dispatched into town carrying money bags to the bank. We feel almost like cartoon figures holding little sacks with dollar signs marked on them, trying our best to look inconspicuous. We have no weapons, nothing to defend ourselves with, anyone could smash us over the head or stab us, so easy if only they knew.

My official job now is to go through the files on record and send out notices of call-up to those who have not completed their military service. There are any number of reasons why this might have occurred: an illness, a temporary deferment, someone managing to hive off without permission, someone on permanent AWOL. As a general principle, I feel ambivalent about this duty. If some lucky bastards have managed to escape the army, good luck to them. On the other hand, many of them are apartheid supporters: let the bastards pay the price! In effect, however, principles are beside the point, for the only rule that counts is that if I am caught letting anyone off the hook, it is DB for me, no questions asked. So I follow procedure. I read the files, find miscreants of various description, and take their names to the sergeant: it is research of a kind. That is how I manage to call up one P. Fourie—without realising he is the famous South African boxer Pierre Fourie, just then lining up for his world light-heavyweight title bout with the even more famous American Bob Foster. Naturally, when consternation breaks loose because of it (headlines in the newspapers; the brigadier has called in), Fourie's service is 'deferred' (forever), but I make myself scarce when he comes into the office to discuss it. That too is how I call up George, a Greek neighbour from down the street in Mons Road. George is the biggest and best operator in the army I have ever seen, and within a short space of time he is parking his orange Alfa Romeo on the pavement outside the Drill Hall, and we are ferrying bets to the tote to place on the horses for the sergeant-major. Having won big once (perhaps George had arranged it, who knows), the sergeant-major now begins to lose more and more, and begins to creep around woefully, as if Uriah Heep had fused with Mr Micawber, always believing the next horse would come in.

In short order, George became a two-stripe corporal, and persuaded me to take one stripe as well, though I had vowed to remain a private forever. The step up gave us just that little extra freedom to gallivant even more. In effect, I was AWOL much of the time now—whenever, in fact, I wasn't in the office or actively on duty. Sometimes I would organise this semi-legally. Because my sarge ran the regimental bar, I became his barman, serving drinks when there'd be a special event on a Friday night. Afterwards, he would always sign a pass for me, so there I would be, heading home for the weekend, to appear miraculously back at work on Monday morning. When I think of it now, I wonder how I did it—but that was the strange blue night of a universe we inhabited, with its own warped habits and altered laws. Such was my temerity that after a while, if I had guard duty on the weekend, I would park my white Ford Anglia, which I had inherited from my aunt, around the corner at a parking lot. And then, for those hours when I was not actually standing guard, I would sometimes drive home, despite my strong impression—perhaps accurate, perhaps not—that the statutory penalty for going AWOL while on duty was death by firing squad. Even when I was actually standing guard, like everyone else I would slither off, find a place to curl up and go to sleep. Or, I would bring my Dostoevsky, reading *Crime and Punishment* completely absorbed, suppressing any awareness that what I was doing was, in the eyes of the South African state, naturally a crime to be followed, if discovered, by severe punishment.

One Friday night, perhaps under the influence of my reading, the world opened up in another way, as if I were standing on a precipice. I was serving as barman as usual, and the guest of honour

156

for a most ostentatious event was Magnus Malan, chief of the
Defence Force and future minister of defence. As the eminent guests
gathered and circulated in their elegant dress uniforms and sashes,
their wives preening on their arms, it felt like Russia somewhere
in the nineteenth century. It was my Dostoevsky moment, *Crime
and Punishment* par excellence. I consciously had the thought: I
am this close and could shoot him. This could be the blow I strike
against apartheid, the ultimate existential choice, and life, if I live,
will be different forever. But of course I didn't shoot anyone, not
only because I wasn't that mad or brave but because my rifle was
somewhere else, and in any case they never gave us any bullets, and
you could see exactly why.

⌒ 38

There was a new conscript at the Drill Hall named Michael. He had gone to school at St John's, but no matter, he was a decent person, and we got on well. He had also recently lost his father, which added a certain poignance to his presence. One weekend, the two of us were assigned to the Carlton Centre, the most flashy and elaborate modern skyscraper in downtown Johannesburg. The army had some kind of public relations or recruiting installation there, and it was our job to watch over it at night. I remember camping out behind the scenes at the Centre in a narrow corridor with enormously high walls, and so desperate was I for intellectual input that I had brought my high-school Latin books with me, immersing myself one more time in the details of Greek mythology and the myriad intricacies of conjugation and declension, subjunctive and deponent verb. The mythology had its own resonance, especially in that building: was I not in the very depths of the labyrinth, the army itself the hulking minotaur, and which blessed Ariadne would offer me the thread to find my way out?

Meanwhile, the general madness and absurdity continued. One night, on guard duty across the road from the Drill Hall, I had just come off my shift—it must have been prime time, six to eight in the evening—and was contemplating my good fortune as I settled down on one of the beds in the guard-house when I heard the guard commander talking on the phone—*liewe Jesus*, or some such equivalent, and yes we'll send someone. Then they look up the roster and my name is called. I try my old ruse from avoiding Hebrew lessons: pretend to be asleep, scrunch up the eyes, dive under the blankets, if they can't find you they will send someone else. But no, they find me and drag me out, and along with a couple of MPs I am to be sent to Kempton Park, my ancestral home no less, where some poor bloody *troepie* has lost his mind and tried to kill everyone, by the sound of it with an axe. He is in the *kas*—the lock-up—there, and we are to bring him back to the *kas* here: I am to be the guard. We go there in terror, and on arrival find mayhem indeed, a bar with everything smashed, alcohol and blood on the floor. And then the soldier is produced for us to return, looking desperate. The MPs have everything worked out: they will be up front, securely protected by the wire mesh in the van; I will be in the back, along with the prisoner. I object vociferously: I don't even have a weapon beyond my bayonet, which the madman will probably use to kill me. But no, they respond, there is no room up front, they are the assigned driver and co-driver, and I am the guard. So, I get in the back, shifting into a corner as far from the axeman as I can. But he is quite broken, and tells me a tale of abuse—how he was bullied relentlessly, and always had to stand guard in some freezing tower miles away. Finally he had lost it and gone after those bastards with everything he could find. By the time we got back to Johannesburg he was weeping on my shoulder, I had my arm around him, and I was more sorry for him than anyone he might have attacked.

It's a Friday afternoon, just before closing, the most dangerous time of the week. Everyone has his plans and is in a heightened state of anxiety because this is exactly when passes can be cancelled, new orders given, or they will find some way to wreck our lives once again. It is the most lethal time when treachery hovers like a blade about to plunge into the ribs. Suddenly the word goes out: we *troepies* are required to assemble in the regimental sergeant-major's office right away. Anxiety levels go even higher, but not for me because I am on guard duty for the weekend—it can't get worse!

So, there in the office the punctilious, upright RSM, his immaculate pencil-moustache aquiver, announces: he needs a volunteer. Unease spreads through the assembled, and there is silence. Again, he needs a volunteer for the weekend, and so, after a while, my hand goes up; I have nothing to lose and something may come out of this. '*Goed*, Clingman'—he says—'but *sant-majoor*,' I say, 'only thing, I am on guard duty this weekend.' 'No problem,' he says, 'guard duty cancelled for you'—and he gives it to someone else who had a pass and now wants to kill me. The RSM tells me to report to his house at camp in Doornkop, which I haven't been back to for ages. When I make my way to the house, the sergeant-major explains in a confiding sort of way that his daughter has been hounding him (where is this going, I wonder), that she wants to go to the circus, that the last time they went there his car was broken into, and, in short, will I come along with them and guard the car while they are away? How can I refuse, not only because it is the RSM but also because this is rather large-scale abuse, and can only do me good. So I go along, sleep in the car while they go into the big tent for the circus, and afterwards the RSM drops me off in town near Loveday Street where I catch a bus home. No pass, no questions asked. On Monday morning, however, pandemonium breaks loose and we are summoned to the RSM's office once again. It turns out that on the weekend the MPs made a snap raid in camp and everyone was AWOL—a huge problem not only for us but for the RSM. He goes through us all one by one, checking for valid passes—but not me. I am in the charmed circle of his own transgression, and therefore quite safe. Yet even those he catches manage to slip away. One says, 'But *sant-majoor*, you gave me a pass, I'll show you,' and heads back to his office to fetch it. There he forges a signature, smudges it under water, and says his passbook accidentally got into the wash on the weekend. It is a truly feeble story, but the RSM accepts it nonetheless—one less piece of explaining for him to do.

One night I am standing guard at Doornkop, as I must have done quite a bit. I am outside the wire and across the road from Soweto, where there is a huge commotion, voices, dogs barking, everything. I have a rifle of course, but as usual no bullets, and quite possibly no bayonet either. It is very unsettling. At last the guard commander comes by on his round, a superannuated PF who, approaching sixty-five but looking ninety-five, is still a corporal, which tells you how low he must be. 'What the hell is going on over there?' he asks me between what is left of his teeth. We stop and listen for a bit to the gathering wave of sound which seems to be heading right for us. '*Weet nie*—don't know—*korporaal*,' I say. He listens to the sound again; the night is pregnant with possibilities, none of them happy. 'Well,' he says, 'let me tell you what to do.' I am expecting a speech on bravery, getting a message through at all costs, holding up the hordes, but that is not what comes. 'If you hear anything,' the corporal tells me, 'anything at all, *hardloop net vir jou vokken lewe, hoor!*'—'Just run for your fucking life, you hear me!' As for the corporal, it didn't look as if he could run anywhere.

At the very last, however, the army nearly gets me. I am just a week away from *klaaring out*—clearing out—and don't want anything to go amiss, so one night I catch the truck back from the Drill Hall to camp, to be safe. I haven't been there in months, and barely know if my *kas* and *trommel* are where I left them. When I get to my tent it is after ten, and someone is sleeping on my bed. *On*, rather than in, because there is a difference. It is an Afrikaner named Theuns, a one-stripe corporal like me, and I know exactly what he is doing. He is sleeping on *my* bed so he won't mess up his own, and he is sleeping *on* it so he can simply smooth it over in the morning. He is a strange one, this: he claims he has almost no sweat glands, which is why he doesn't need to shower, which he seldom does. At any rate, I kick Theuns off my bed, he shuffles off mumbling to his own, and I go to sleep. The next morning, back at work, I get sudden word:

I must bring my beret and report instantly to the RSM. My circus tricks with his family are now apparently forgotten, and I must be in trouble. I run all over the Drill Hall looking for Theuns: he is my alibi, the only one who can vouch for the fact that I was in camp. How fortunate I had to wake him up and kick him off my bed! But I can't find him anywhere, and hurry breathlessly to the RSM's office—to find Theuns already standing there. I start to speak to him, but the RSM shooshes me. He draws us both to attention and then asks Theuns, 'Where did you sleep last night?' 'In Clingman's bed, *sant-majoor*,' says Theuns. 'And you, Clingman, where did you sleep?' 'In my bed, *sant-majoor*, Theuns saw me because I kicked—' Enough! RSM won't let me finish. 'Right,' he says, 'we're off to see the major.'

Quick march off to the major, screech to a halt outside his door. RSM goes in, comes out, quick-march inside, screech to a halt in front of his desk, stand to attention. RSM mounts his allegation. There was a raid in camp last night, both Theuns and Clingman marked absent. Theuns says he was in Clingman's bed, and Clingman also says he was in his bed. 'So what I want to know, major, is whether we charge them both for being AWOL, or the two of them for sleeping together!' I almost burst out laughing, and the major asks me to explain, so I do, at which point you can just about see the RSM crumple. The major gives us an obligatory five-minute homily on responsibility (apparently he expects better from one-stripe corporals), then it is about-turn, door open, quick-march, screech to a halt outside. The RSM, livid, berates us both under his breath. '*Ja, julle twee,*' he says. '*Julle kakstories mag goed genoeg vir die majoor wees, maar nie vir my nie!*' ('Your bullshit stories may be good enough for the major, but not for me!')

This is my goodbye to the army. In any case, Theuns was hardly appetising.

39 ⤸

If I re-entered the army a free man, I came out an alien being.

How did he feel, this person whose planetary origins were uncertain? For one thing, he knew about complicity, about its reality, its undeniability. He had been in the army, he had served a regime he abhorred. He was caught there between an old model—whites who had served honourably during the Second World War, his father among them—and a new one, in which service involved the maintenance of apartheid. The older generation, by and large, had not caught up with the difference and didn't know how to support us, and those of us who knew the difference, yet complied anyway, had to live with an acute form of self-awareness. We resisted in minor ways, formal and informal, everything from throwing bed-frames off a sky-high pile in an aircraft hangar to going AWOL, yet not everyone did so in the same way, and our very presence fed the beast that was living off our bodies and minds.

So, henceforth a certain kind of shame, no talk about the army, not something to be proud of at all. And, though much of it was absurd and even funny, a small vow not to forget how miserable and awful it really was. But there is also now a kind of knowledge that runs deeper because of it, and certain questions. How many systems are we a part of? Where do choice and resistance begin? He has learned what some will never see, that one person's privilege here is profoundly connected with another's disprivilege there. This is a reality intensified in and because of the South African system,

163

but its resonance is global. There is no escaping this knowledge, and henceforth everything will take place with it in mind. Yet is he a joiner, an opponent? That is another question, for his imprint is different. What takes place will go by another route, another current, and he knows that should he be called to account by the Great Judgement in the sky, he may never be able to excuse it. Possibly he will not even try, but simply hold up his hands in acknowledgement. Guilty, I am guilty and forever will be. But if nothing I can do will ever be sufficient, how far does my obligation reach, just how much will ever be enough? Even framing the question in that way brings its own kind of horror, for what is the calculus of 'enough' in the face of pain and injustice in the world?

On one level alienation comes because he is out of cycle. His friends have all left the army a year ago. They have been at university, leading lives of freedom and commitment. He joins them in Cape Town at the end of the year, and finds he has nothing to say. He has been away, and now the world seems almost entirely false. He withdraws, he becomes unfriendly, even cruel, at times the beast himself. At home his father is in his chair, unmoving, while his mother presides over a household of servants. A kind of silence has descended. Are they not all horrified by the lives they are living? Is everyone suffering from their own kind of depression? His brother is still living at home, making his way as a musician, but he—he just wants to get out, get away, and it seems impossible. One day he stares at his hands and weeps. He feels those hands can do so much, but what is it, what is it that they can do?

At fourteen he knew he wanted to be a doctor; he had the healing spirit, felt even that he had healing hands. He announced his decision at the time to his mother, who hung onto it as her very hope even as she tried not to interfere. Now he has been accepted at medical school, both in Johannesburg and Cape Town. But he has become corrupted by the idea of purity—pure ideas, pure thought, pure study, pure search for pure meaning, and so he will be going to university for a degree in the humanities. History will be part of it, because he is convinced there is more to it than they learned at school, and this will be a form of revenge (he can see himself in tweed jacket, with pipe, at an advancing age). He will also take English, because he might as well, and Philosophy for the sheer thought of it, and Latin because the Classics were his first love, the idea of Delphi as the centre of the universe on a Mediterranean mountain a shimmering promise filled with the scent of thyme and rosemary. If his spirit has migrated anywhere, it is there.

He is an existentialist still, this boy, fragile, trying to make his way. Everything becomes a matter of choice: how long you lie in bed after the alarm has rung (he counts to ten, then gets up), how you approach your work (he will hold nothing back, present himself with total commitment), how much you eat, how much your body needs. He who once lived so much in his body is now starting to live in his mind. He will sit outside on the grass studying the ants, marvelling at their industry and purpose, pondering relative scales of small and large. He would love to have a girlfriend, but doesn't know how (he has been cruel and thoughtless on more than one occasion). He eats less and less meat, and then less and less altogether, so that he becomes a vegetarian who is barely eating at all. What is all that about? Some of it is ineffable, but he has seen the world of bodies and muscle, of armies and strength and mindless meaninglessness. Anorexia is not a word that leaves anyone's lips, indeed it may barely exist as a word at the time; later he will be interested to see it is a condition that applies mainly to girls. But he is a girl-boy then, withdrawing, finding his inner image and never being satisfied. He is becoming lighter, airier, purer, he is curious to see how everything slows down, not only the rhythms of the body but seemingly the lineaments of time. His family is bemused, concerned, and sometimes he is mocked for his vegetarian ways. He holds out, nothing can touch him. His dreams are of flying.

And then some time during the year there is crisis. He collapses, and the doctor is called, and gives him an ultimatum. You, my boy, have to eat, and you have to eat meat, or you are going to die. So he does. He gives up and returns to the world, though he will always choose around questions of food. Afterwards there is a feeling that never leaves: he has compromised once again. Just where and how does one draw the line of being in the world?

My first-year courses were chosen, and I began. How did it feel?
It felt many things at once: strange, exciting, foreign, but also an
opening, a portal I approached with an air of awe and veneration.
Neither of my parents had been to university. My father wasn't that
way inclined, and after school had entered the Air Force, training
as a navigator just as the war was ending. My mother wanted to be
in the world, and had started with secretarial jobs in Johannesburg.
Neither of my uncles on my father's side had been to university; on
my mother's there were the uncles by marriage, the two doctors and
a lawyer, but theirs was a different part of the cosmos. My mother's
sisters had gone on to higher education: the eldest, Hilda, a woman
of sharp mind and tremendous moral clarity, had trained to be a
teacher; Cissie, who died young, was a brilliant lawyer, and ran the
foreign relations section of the South African Red Cross during the
Second World War; Sheila had wanted to study physics, but that was
not a field for a woman. The four sisters, each in her own way, had
given up their aspirational lives to their husbands. But somewhere in
there, I saw that opening. When I was at school, I had gone with my
family to the university to hear my cousin Mark play clarinet solo
in an orchestra. As we approached the Greek columns of the Great
Hall, I had felt my distance and smallness but also the grandeur
of the setting. When we left, somewhere inside was the feeling, or
perhaps it was a question: I want to go there, is that a place where I
could belong?

But for now I didn't know how to, and fumbled around. In Philosophy, where the first-year class was way too large, the professors suddenly switched from Plato to Logic, which instantly got rid of half the students, at which point they switched back to Plato: quite a logical strategy. English I just didn't get for a while; at school we had counted images in *Macbeth*, but here I didn't really know what was wanted. Sadly, my Latin classes were as boring as a Sunday parking lot: rote learning of the worst kind, and my revenge in the end-of-year exam was to regurgitate word for word the life of Catullus that had been recited to us in lecture. For which of course I got a first: their irony beat my irony. History felt like a challenge one could go into and into, and yet there was something about its narratives that didn't quite satisfy. By second year, however, I was suddenly *there*: I knew what it was all about and what to do. In English, as time went on, I invented for myself a form of structuralism—which I realised afterwards when I found a book by Roland Barthes in the library—and virtually every one of my essays was a structural analysis of meaning, whether in a poem by Gerard Manley Hopkins or Charles Dickens's *Bleak House*. In History one of the professors quoted me in a lecture on whether the Lisbon earthquake of 1755 had prompted the end of the Enlightenment or whether the response to it was merely a symptom of the shift. By the end of the year I had achieved firsts in each of my four courses, which was quite unusual. Fortunately for my sense of reality, when the results came out (we went to the Great Hall to see our names on the boards) I was working for a bookie at an off-tote betting agency—my army experience coming in handy. There, amidst the drunks and derelicts losing all their money on the horses, the bookie didn't give a damn about university, and managed to mock both me and my friend Anthony, who had got me the job, when the numbers didn't add up at the end of the day. *Ja*, four firsts, and *still* you can't count!

168

Underneath it all was still the old current, the existential one. Most of all this stranger, this alien, wished to turn aside from what he thought of as mere smartness. Smartness was about brains, but there was something else that was about meaning. He wanted depth, not to be 'smart', and firmly believed that was where his good results came from. This meant too a belief in the deeper route, that if one took the right way for its own reasons, results would come of their own accord, and you could trust them. Somewhere along the way he discovered Martin Buber—perhaps late, but he discovered him— and the notion of pure relation, the I–Thou, captured his being. He applied it, as far as he could, to everything—to people, to trees, to his work. So, in approaching a literary text, or a historical or philosophical problem, first of all you had to *be* there—to present yourself, in full relation. Then the text or the problem would speak its secrets, open itself up, as you did, and the writing would follow. The writing too was a matter of relation, of presenting yourself to your subject matter, which would equally present itself to you. With some variation, this was an approach he continued to follow.

As a sign of his spiritual orientation he learned to stand on his hands for long minutes at a time. The world upside down or right side up: what did it matter, he was free, the light body in perfect balance, alternative to the body of the world around him, pure air. An image came to him, which he drew, of a tightrope walker on a rope across a chasm, yet the difference was that the rope was not fixed but unfolded before the figure as he walked. The step invoked the path, it was a matter of faith and belief and risk—what he liked to call the precariousness of it all. Or there was an image of a piano balanced crosswise on a tightrope, with the pianist sitting on a stool before it, playing in the perfect equipoise and contemplative attention it required. It was fragile, he was fragile, he may have been romantic, he was certainly romantic, but this was who he was, and at some stratum of his life, though distant now, who he is.

169

He is in third year, his last, and one of his favourite teachers, Lorraine, has called him in to have a chat. He has written an essay for her on *Middlemarch*, and she has given it an unheard-of mark, a 93. She tells him she would have marked it higher, but it simply wouldn't have been accepted in the department. She also tells him, you understand people, would you think of working with people, perhaps psychiatry? His response is an immediate no, he wants to carry on doing what he is doing, discovering, taking it further. In that case, she says, you must go overseas to study once you are finished here, because you can do very good things. He leaves Lorraine's office essay in hand, understanding for the first time what the phrase 'walking on air' actually means. He is in a kind of delirium, an exhilaration. He sees his friend Rory over there, walking across the piazza towards the Great Hall. Oh Rory, he calls out, come here, I have to tell you what happened. But Rory has come up of his own accord, and is speaking at the same time, saying, have you heard what happened? There are riots in Soweto and all hell has broken loose, and look at those helicopters flying overhead. It is 16 June 1976.

41

The university in Johannesburg had a proud record when it came to questions of justice. Growing up, we had read in the newspapers about the generation of students which had preceded us, protesting against the racial decrees of apartheid and the apparatus of the growing police state. Leaders in NUSAS—the National Union of South African Students—had risked arrest, had been arrested, had spoken out when it counted. There was an aura about these students—their clarity, their dignity, their courage, the forthright quality of their voices. But they were living under the rules of a different era, even as it transformed. Now it was a much darker age as the conventions of the past made way for the hall-of-mirrors world of torture, death in detention, and the blunt will to power of those who ruled with ruthlessness and without restraint. A few years later and Neil Aggett, a former student and dedicated young doctor, was killed. How many could or would be like him? The risks were real and severe, and any moment in the dark night of every day could prompt the inspection of conscience and the recognition of failure, for most of us, to live up to it.

The atmosphere on campus was eerie, uncanny. It was a hugely political time, with great dramas unfolding not only in South Africa but elsewhere in the region. FRELIMO came to power in Mozambique, displacing the Portuguese colonial overlords, and it felt the white edifice of the whole of southern Africa might shift. Carlos, who came from Mozambique, would be up on his soapbox proclaiming in his Portuguese accent, '*Everything* is political, *birth* is political, *death* is political, your mother's *womb* is political!' He, a profound liberationist, was later murdered in Maputo exploring corruption in the same FRELIMO movement he had supported. On the lawns in front of the student union a fellow who called himself Kropotkin wandered round with scraggly hair and beard. We would sit on those lawns at lunchtime eating floppy chips from the cafeteria, and every conversation was preceded by a glance over the shoulder to see who might be listening, for there were spies everywhere; the arts of discretion, of strategic silence and gesture became second nature. At one point there was some estimation that a majority of members on the Students' Representative Council were police spies. One of them, vice-president of the SRC and a member of the national executive of NUSAS, was secretly a police officer and agent provocateur, enlisting students in anti-apartheid activities to entrap them. Later he was responsible for the assassination by car-bomb of major figures such as Ruth First and Jeannette Schoon, as well as Schoon's six-year-old daughter, Katryn. Some twenty years after, following his amnesty by the Truth and Reconciliation Commission, he walked freely in the streets of Johannesburg.

How to negotiate your way through it all? On the one hand you want to live your life, study well and hard, explore your existence. And yet, there is a need to do something. From the black campuses the ethos is challenging, for black students are now opposed not only to the apartheid regime but also to whites who want to help them. Distantly, we hear of the new philosophy. It's called Black Consciousness, and its chief exponent is a brilliant and forceful young man named Steve Biko. Blacks must free themselves, that is the logic, and the first step is to free their minds, because one cannot be conscious and at the same time a slave. Whites who speak for you are not your friends; they are part of the system they claim to oppose, because they are stealing your voice, representing you,

172

displacing you once again. Whites who oppose apartheid must find their own way, and their own reasons, to do it. But patronage towards blacks is unacceptable, and liberals are almost worse than the Nationalists because of the duplicity involved. We hear these things, and at first it seems an ironic joke, something that might have been crafted by the masters of apartheid, a form of nationalism, a separatism. And it flies in the face of the non-racial philosophy of the ANC. But the ANC is almost gone now, its leaders are all overseas or in prison, and here is a new generation who object to the tolerance of their elders almost as much as they do to whites. It takes a while for this to sink in, before we see the nature and even necessity of the shift. We must learn to support but not speak for, to listen instead of talk, to accept that role for the foreseeable future and maybe forever.

We look around—I look around—for some way to contribute. I attend a NUSAS seminar on the miners' strike of 1922—the famous one my grandfather had been called out, if need be, to suppress, when white miners attacked blacks and wanted the workers of the world to fight and unite for a white South Africa. The seminar is meant to focus on a particular debate: was this strike about class or race? But when the audience—and we are an audience of only two—begin to say that, based on the facts, it looks as if race played a prominent part, the student leader loses patience because that is the wrong answer, and prods us towards the correct one, ignoring the kind of gymnastic contortions one would have to perform to get there. Hmmm, perhaps that is how black students feel about being patronised. When the seminar ends, though I have heard the majestic call of NUSAS, I decide to look around for something else.

I find it in a student voluntary organisation run, more or less, by my friends from school, David and Clive. David started as an engineer but has switched to law; Clive is taking a Bachelor of Commerce degree but is not your average business student. The organisation works with black communities in rural areas, building schools and clinics. In all this the rules are clear: we provide charity for no one; we respond to communities who approach us rather than the other way round; our activities must be collaborative, so that communities work together with us. There will be no providing *for*; we have learned that much. I head out with others in winter to Thaba Bosiu, the Mountain at Night, in Lesotho, where we are building a clinic. The sun is angled, the nights high and cold and brilliantly clear. I take pleasure in mixing the cement, the *dagha*, not to be confused with marijuana, *dagga*, which is in plentiful supply, though I myself am not partial to it. The skilled among us can take a shovel full of *dagha*, and curl it through the air to land just where needed as the breeze blocks are being laid. We eat copious thick slices of bread and peanut butter, warming hands on mugs of coffee in the morning; we travel in trucks and VW Kombis and listen to the Dutch group Focus playing their wild rock ululations on tape. For diversion we go horse-riding, and one of our group, quite striking in his beauty, goes bareback in both senses—shirtless and without a saddle, long hair streaming behind him as he gallops down the mountainside.

Back in Johannesburg at the university, someone pays us a visit. He has come from another campus, and likes what we do, feels we can expand elsewhere. If we are interested he has access to funding, he says. We listen, a room full of people, and ask him to leave while we discuss the matter. When he walks out and closes the door, the verdict to some is clear enough, though I haven't seen it immediately, because as usual I am far too naive, far too trusting. He is a spy, and we will have nothing to do with him, a decision which is affirmed when his name comes up in the Truth and Reconciliation proceedings many years later.

42 ⌇

On 16 June 1976, all was suspended. There I was with my friend
Rory. Minutes before I had been contemplating unheralded opportunity, making my way overseas, exploring all I would be able to
explore. If my parents had never been to university, if others around
me came with an enviable background in that respect, this was new,
my private dedication opening up a path I could never have foreseen.
It seemed that I could actually do things; it was a validation I
had never dared to imagine. And then here comes Rory with his
news, and up there are the helicopters, and slowly the commotion
around us begins to take shape as groups of students gather to share
information, work out what is happening. We have known about
the campaign against compulsory instruction in Afrikaans in black
schools, about planned demonstrations, but things have suddenly
escalated unbelievably. What are we to do? How are we to make our
presence felt, have an impact, show our solidarity?

The next day I remember, or imagine remembering, a mass
meeting in the Great Hall, held indoors because open-air meetings
were banned. Or perhaps we simply made our way to Jan Smuts
Avenue, the traditional site of our protests. Through these years we
had been there many times, under increasingly restrictive conditions.
Students had to stand some distance apart from one another (the
law on illegal gatherings); we were not allowed to move or march
off campus. So that was how we usually stood, still and apart, white
drivers hooting as they went by, police watching and filming from

the divide across the way, others taking photographs. We assumed there were police files and records on most of us. The police dogs would be there too, snapping and yanking at their chains, and every now and again someone would be bitten. And there was tear gas, always tear gas, just in case the police felt like making us run. We would stand alone, mute, largely impotent, yet we would stand there nonetheless.

But today—today is different. For lo and behold, when we get to the grass verge on Jan Smuts Avenue, slowly we realise: there are no police here, no films, no photographs, no batons, no tear gas, no dogs. Where have they all gone? The helicopters flying overhead towards the south provide an answer: they are all in Soweto. They have been caught off guard, all their forces are required in the townships, and we are on our own. The feeling is quite vertiginous: now we have to decide what to do with our freedom. Slowly we move together, coalesce, and then a murmur runs through the crowd: we are going to march into the centre of Johannesburg. This is uncertain territory, we are nervous, but the black children in Soweto are facing police guns, and this is little enough by comparison. We edge off campus, heading south along Jan Smuts Avenue, crossing Queen Elizabeth Bridge towards the city centre. Now along with the vertigo there is exhilaration and also determination. We are singing and chanting, many with fists raised in the Black Consciousness salute and slogan: *Amandla! Awethu!* Power to the People! (Are there any others, like me, who ponder how appropriate it is for whites to use it even as we are caught up in the momentum?) As we reach the city centre we march right down the middle of the streets, a great mass of us, and some black workers join us for stretches of the way. Others look down on us from high buildings, and we don't know how to interpret their silence. No one has seen this in many years, no one knows what it means.

We reach the Library gardens, and there is puzzlement, for we have got here, it is an unbidden destination of a kind, but now what should we do? Some advocate staying on the loose in the city centre, others continuing the march back to campus. Leaders confer, and the march takes off again, but it is a mistake. We have circled through town and reached Jorissen Street in Braamfontein, approaching the university once more, but we have not noticed others secretly joining our ranks. It is winter, and they are men in olive greatcoats. We march now in gathering confidence and relief, for safe territory— the territory that normally confined us—is now in sight, and we even begin to break up a little. And then, at a signal, the men who have joined us open up their coats, revealing chains and crowbars beneath. The police may have been occupied elsewhere, but they have called in their natural allies, the white railway workers, who now set about us with a vengeance. They swing their chains and crowbars wildly, hitting anyone in their path. Everyone scatters, people scream and flee, run into shops for safety. In all the mayhem my friend Colin kicks a bus, but he is wearing clogs, and his clog gets caught in the petrol cap housing as the bus takes off down the road. Colin loses his shoe, and starts hopping back to campus; thus are the great moments in history punctuated. Others are not so lucky. Someone is badly beaten and wounded, and we try to take him into a pharmacy for refuge. But the pharmacist closes his doors, he does not want us in there. This crunching of flesh and bone is the real thing, no questions asked.

As always, we know the difference: no one has died here, unlike Soweto. The afternoon newspapers are beginning to shout their headlines about the day's events there. A young boy, Hector Pieterson, has been shot, and there will be more; schoolchildren are facing real bullets. On our campus there is another meeting, and a decision to march again that afternoon. But it is a mistake to announce such things in advance, and in my own particular mood—look where the morning had begun for me, look where it ended—I feel a certain depression and futility, and don't go along. That afternoon the police are smarter. They allow the march to leave the campus, but when it reaches the bridge they seal off first one end and then the other, trapping the students. And then the police and railway workers attack once again, and students are running down the side of the bridge, leaping off parapets trying to get away. Even for us we are in a new world, and no one knows how or where it will end.

43

Windows, the window to my room. When I was fourteen or so, I found a sticker and used its letters and decorative flourishes to fashion my initials, SRC, with a circle around them. This I stuck on my window. At night, against the dark, they showed luminous, white. As I see it now, the window I was looking through was me, my initials on its surface. The window was a membrane between myself and the world; a circle around the self, white circle against the dark. It was a membrane that allowed me through, but it also let the outside in, and at night that outside could be threatening. Sometimes at night we would hear footsteps running down the side of the house. When I went to sleep I knew just how close my head was to the window, and my mind was a symbolic landscape. Usually the window was open above me, fastened with its butterfly screw, but anyone could undo that screw, reach in or just smash the window entirely, the meagre bars no defence. Nightmares of intrusion took hold, men in the room in my sleep, and I was paralysed, a sudden cold feeling in my flesh, I could not raise my voice to cry out. It was a matter of daring to sleep every night; the window was also within, and it let my subconscious out.

I remember other dreams, from earlier on. In one I am falling from a tremendous height towards our garden. I have been jettisoned from a plane, and am trying to open a parachute. It flies out above me but will not open, and there is our garden growing larger, its high jacaranda trees rushing towards me. There is nothing for it; I steel myself and resolve to grab onto a branch as I go by. I do so, but as I take hold of the branch it dissolves in my hands, and here comes the ground rushing towards me, no escape. But as I hit the ground I too dissolve; it happens quite naturally, and that is when I wake up. The dream is repeated so often that I get to know its routines like a script, so that the end which used to cause such panic becomes predictable even in my sleep. Later, after the army, after South Africa, when I am studying in England, my dreams are all of war, of fleeing across battlefields with bullets and explosions all around, and we have to get somewhere, but of course we can't, and the sensation is of turmoil without end.

Thank goodness for those other, quite different dreams when as danger approaches I suddenly take off and fly. I reach out my arms like wings, and there it is, I can lift, levitate and soar above it all, above everyone, tipping my hands and arms ever so slightly this way and that to control my arc through the sky. Everything falls away behind me; it is the easiest thing in the world, something I know I can do, a sensation of pure exhilaration.

Day stories, night stories, the ones we see and the ones we do not. History is buried in the psyche. Multiply this by hundreds, thousands, millions of people in every corner of the globe, in every century. What were the dreams of those who experienced the very worst trauma? And the dreams of those who inflicted it? Auschwitz, Belsen, Rwanda, Tuol Sleng, Steve Biko, Neil Aggett: who will write a true history of human dreams?

For each of us, our lives construct our dreams. We build our walls against them, but the walls become the form of our entrapment, prompting the very dreams we are trying to escape. That is why it is so hard to cry out, to get out of the rooms we are in, our initials written on the windows, the eyes we see through. These are our dreams, our hauntings, and the only question they ask is, what are we going to do?

180

44

Life continues in its own way. In our voluntary organisation we
hold meetings, believe small is beautiful, and under the guidance
of our engineering and architectural friends develop mechanisms
of what we call appropriate technology—technology suited to its
environment, its ecology. I go to a student conference in Durban
where the NUSAS leaders arrive—and leave—like rock stars. Prime
Minister Vorster, former minister of justice, former internee during
the war as a Nazi sympathiser, wags his finger, mandates torture and
threatens general doom. At university we go to the film club, and in
the suburbs there are private clubs too, where banned movies are
shown by subscription. Some of them show naked bodies, and in
someone's garage I see *A Clockwork Orange*. There, staring back at
me off the screen, is an eye with long lashes circled in black much
like my own, while its owner instructs his droogies in the finer arts of
mayhem. In truth I am jealous: is it so easy to vaunt your flamboyant
eye? At Mangles, where my brother plays guitar, we listen to folk
music, and at the Market Theatre witness new forms of drama
where your sensibilities are assailed and you leave feeling lacerated
and spent. People talk the new politics of the day, the new theories,
Althusser, Arrighi and Saul, and drop dark hints of the underground.
My friend Rory saves up all his essay assignments to write in one
night, and blasts Jimi Hendrix out over the garden as he finishes in
his room at five in the morning. At an open-air music festival a black
companion from our exchange to America arrives, and needs a lift

181

home to Soweto. Late on a Sunday night I drop him off, and become completely lost in the maze of the gargantuan township where the streets have numbers but no names. When I go into a store to ask for help, the men there look at me with disbelief and ask if I am trying to get myself killed. But one of them goes outside to his car and drives ahead, showing me the way out.

He is still a loner, this boy working his way through it all, though he has his desires and needs. One day a soccer match is arranged—students versus professors—and he plays for the first time in a decade. Afterwards, one of the girls who have been watching says, you always look so thin, but you have very good legs! There are girls of course, and always have been, both at school and also on campus. One was very kind, and he ended up being cruel; one draws him into the mystique of her existence, but she has a steady boyfriend, and he feels tagged along (when a similar situation comes along later, he draws on his experience and turns it down). One is super-smart and has an apartment of her own; it works for a while, and sometimes he stays over, and he drives around the country with her too, but then it falls apart. One he brings home for a joyful interlude on the carpet in front of the fire in the living room while his parents are down the passageway, behind closed doors, asleep.

His friends have begun to move out of home into communes, and then later to Crown Mines, a former mining area to the south of the city where they set up something like a settlement. Whenever he can, he gets out of the house, once to house-sit for a professor, and then to do the same at his friends' house in Doornfontein when they are away. Doornfontein is the suburb where many Jews lived when they first set up in Johannesburg at the turn of the twentieth century; now it is run-down, dingy, a place for derelicts and drunkards in the streets. He reads his books there, studying, but then heads out because he needs company. He goes to Honey Street in Berea, where a commune has been established, home to some eight or nine people. Once it was the Universal Church—a new-age religious centre—but now it houses students who live together, eat together, sometimes sleep together, and where, if you are taking a bath, someone will come in and use the toilet. When he arrives on this particular night, there is no one home except Moira, whom he finds lying on her bed reading the collected poems of W.B. Yeats. He had met Moira before, in Cape Town when he came out of the army, with her boyfriend of the time, and neither had paid the other much attention. But W.B. Yeats—what an amazing thing! For he has fallen in love with the poems of Yeats, with their music, their sonority, their mythic resonance and—for a budding structuralist such as him—their extraordinary form. He has even begun to write Yeats-esque poems, heavy, ponderous, beating. Moira hadn't read Yeats much before, and she didn't read him much after, but, as she said, her timing was good.

Moira left Pretoria to come to university in Johannesburg; she is an art student, and her room has the most beautiful stained-glass bay window. What shall we do, we are alone, no one around, let's go out, so they do, to a very strange place called the Johannesburger that serves food tasting just like its name, and quite a lot to drink. And then it's back to Doornfontein where he is staying, and something has begun, slowly at first, but then they are together day and night. He loves the feel of Moira's cheeks, her spirit, her sparkiness, something ineffable that he doesn't question but just feels right. She, she just takes him as he is. Her name is Moira Miller, and one of her artist friends calls her Moira Mirror; she becomes a different kind of mirror to him. She doesn't see his birthmark, she sees him as decorated, speckled, and says so. He brings her home on a Friday night and his mother tells her, it's all right, we're eating fish, so you don't have to worry; she had thought Moira was Catholic, and goes weak at the knees when she finds out she is Jewish.

He is now in his honours year, and has been accepted to study overseas; he will be leaving in a few months. Moira is uncertain, unsure—why extend your love when someone is going away and will leave you? But no, he tells her, we must believe, we can make it happen. At night he whirls around with her on the lawns at the university, and they go home to sleep in her cramped single bed. One day, in the garden at home, there is a moment that seems almost other-worldly; he feels his grandmother Rebecca has come there to bless them, the jacaranda canopy enveloping them with its promise and seal. They go camping in the Magaliesberg, and swim in a pool where, in the reflection of the water, striated light radiates from their heads like a halo. In his office at university Moira cuts his long hair, one side at a time. Her mother dies suddenly, unexpectedly, and he holds her hand at the cemetery, meeting her family for the first time, realising he will never in his life meet her mother.

Soon his season has come, and he will be leaving. He sits in the garden with her before they go to the airport, with his new boots for the winter and his short hair. There, once again in the northern hemisphere, he waits near a public telephone booth for her calls. They write letters to each other and keep them. In December, when it is dark at three o'clock, he uses his return ticket to come back to Johannesburg and see her. They travel down to Cape Town, he gets sick in the car on the way back, yet on this trip something has been affirmed. Seven months later she comes to England to join him. They see Bob Dylan wearing his white face at a place called Fleet in the countryside. Afterwards, because transport has broken down, they walk with hundreds of others bleating like sheep along lanes under a moonlit night towards the station. There a train gets them part of the way, but it is now the early hours of Sunday morning and nothing is running. They sleep on a table in the waiting room in Reading.

A few days later they are married. He wears a blue velvet jacket and no tie, and breaks the wedding glass with his clogs; she wears the most beautiful pink dress and straw hat, and high red sandals. The rabbi wants to know if they are bohemian. They have journeyed together ever since.

Double Vision

45

Across time, across space, across perspective, in my mind my daughters (and, through them, their children and children's children, if they have a care to know) are asking me: what was it really like to be there? What was it like to be white, to have servants, to be Jewish in an African land? I cannot answer in the abstract except to say we weren't entirely white because we were Jewish; we weren't entirely Jewish because we were white; and of course we weren't entirely African because we were both Jewish and white. But in the midst of this we were all these things, white, Jewish, African, in our own form, our own guise, our own habits of body and spirit and mind. We were from the southern part of Africa, living there in our own way.

Our Africa was hardly Africa because we had not become indigenous and perhaps never would. But even South Africa as a whole seemed hardly to belong to Africa: the hard boundaries of our system had cut us off. Still, there was the veld, the grasses, the animals, the birds, the stars, the clouds, the skies and the extraordinary red soil of our earth, which still moves me to this day. All left their taste, their scent, their imprint, their footprints on us.

Our servants were our knowledge of Africans, a relationship both intimate and distorted. They knew us in all our habits and sins; we didn't know them except in certain dimensions. All I can say is beware a world where others do for you without your doing for them, where the circle of reciprocity becomes stretched out of human shape. This world of course exists outside South Africa as well.

Being Jewish was to live on the threshold of visibility and invisibility, seeing ourselves and being seen by others. How much did we identify as being Jewish? What does it even mean to be born into an identity? An identity is something that you become, but it has fault-lines within and linkages beyond; being Jewish was there in our lives, but we crossed its boundaries every day. Some Jews had taken up the struggle against apartheid, notably so, so that there was a general suspicion among other whites that communists were Jews and vice versa. There was Baruch in our own family, serving nine years in prison for sabotage. Afrikaners identified with us as God's chosen people—in their most optimistic moments seeing themselves as His chosen people in Africa—but to us the whole idea of being chosen was suspect, unless it meant being chosen to be victimised. And when the Afrikaners saw us in a different way, we were of course a threat, vagrant, untrustworthy types who belonged nowhere and took up subversive political causes. The Anglos saw us sometimes with respect, but sometimes with a silent but unmistakable condescension. And there were of course Jews who, if they didn't fit in perfectly, nonetheless made significant amounts of money out of apartheid and went to synagogue every Saturday. All of this, for everyone, was mediated through particular families, orientations, inward and outward signatures of the self.

To be Jewish in our world was to find the borders not only of visibility but also of silence and sound. Our job was to be not too loud, not too ostentatious, not to offend. White South Africans of our ilk spoke quietly, as if not making too strong a claim on the world, and for Jews it was even more so. We feared our visibility, yet we wanted, like anyone else, to be visible.

How much more so for me with my eye, the very medium and instrument of visibility, the thing that saw, the thing that made me visible in a vulnerable way. It was the mark of who I was, the destiny

I could not, would not, did not even want to escape. It was the mark of being Jewish, it was my whiteness, my blackness, it was my being African, male, female. It was the mark of my tentativeness, my claim. It was and is my very birthmark.

⁓ 46

Seeing here, seeing there: double vision. Seeing left, seeing right: double vision. Seeing then, seeing now: double vision and more. It is seeing through two eyes that gives us our sense of depth as well as space. The stereoscopic view: this is how we measure where we are and where we have been, the very coordinates of our perception. What are the mysteries of vision? Because of my eye, because of my birthmark, for me this is a complicated and interesting question.

It is in this connection that, more than forty-five years after this story began and nine thousand miles from where it began, Dr R is telling me: your left eye is the one controlling everything. I have come to Dr R because for some time I have been concerned about my variable vision, the difference between left and right. But her statement is confusing if not downright absurd, contradicting everything I know or seem to know.

My left eye? How can that be? Over the years it is my left eye that has been eminently the weaker, getting more and more short-sighted (that old plea on a hilltop in the army!), while my right eye has been the strong one, the one that can see at distance. The right eye is the one with the birthmark, so it is weaker in that respect, but concerning its vision there has never been much doubt. Of course the differential has had its uses. For very small print I take off my glasses, close my right eye and bring the page up to my left, while for objects far away the right will suffice. I have learned how to make the most of my gifts.

But now Dr R is telling me the left eye is stronger. She must mean in some other sense, and it turns out she does. It is almost a moral one; the left eye is in control. This is about balance and power.

She tells me more. She says, I am amazed you can even walk, let alone ride a bicycle or play tennis, such is the imbalance in your system. And it puts huge stress on the visual architecture of your mind. For vision is not just about eyes, it is eyes and mind together that assemble and register the image. Most surprising is the fact that you have chosen to work with books, because that makes the strain on your system immense.

Listening to her I am tempted by many things. I am tempted by denial: she must be wrong, how can my left eye be the stronger, it just doesn't make sense! But then, given my symbolic line of work, I am also tempted by allegory. If she is right, then weakness and strength are not opposites but exist in a knot of mutually defined intricacy. Apparent strength may be an expression of weakness, while underlying weakness may have its controlling features. Could I not see my family that way? And what about South Africa itself? Who was strong, who was weak in that tangle? The two terms were totally interconnected.

For the most part, however, I leave allegory alone, because this is my own particular problem, and one I have to deal with. Always I have been focused on my right eye, because of the birthmark. But I have neglected the left, left that side of me out of the equation altogether. Hanging on to what I feared defined me, I had reinforced that definition of my self. So the left eye, neglected, had made do; it saw close up, turned inwards, found its own form of control while my right eye gazed distractedly outwards. I knew orthodox medical philosophy would find this the purest nonsense. But I wasn't concerned with orthodox medical philosophy. For more than ten years I had been looking for an eye doctor who would understand me, who would comprehend how my vision was not just a matter of my lenses but my way of seeing in the world. Now I had found her, and Dr R was telling me: your left eye, which appears weaker, is controlling your vision.

And so she proposes vision therapy to correct the balance, and I am both trepidatious and eager to take it up. What does it involve? Will it work? What will I find? Yet as I understand it, I have nothing to lose, and possibly some things to discover. So I begin the therapy, doing exercises under supervision in Dr R's offices, and also daily on my own at home.

Here are some of the exercises that come to occupy me.

On a card showing what are called 'small lifesavers' (they look just like the coloured lifesavers on the packets), I gaze at paired circles, red and green, at varying distances from one another, and construct a 3D image from the combination of the two in the space between them. Some of the letters in the images recede or stand out in 3D if I am doing it correctly.

I use transparencies of two similar, but much bigger, circles which I affix to a window. These are called 'large lifesavers', and again the idea is to see the 3D image from the two of them as I come closer and then step away. This is an approximation of what they look like; if you gaze at the right with your left eye and the left with your right, you will see it:

They look like eyes looking back and, though because of that it is difficult, they help my eyes to see.

There is also what I think of as bead torture, although later I get used to it. I look at three beads, red, yellow and green, arranged

194

equidistantly along a length of string. As I focus on them in turn, near, middle and far, the string seems to make an X in front of and beyond each one. I move the near bead towards me in steps for convergence and away from me for divergence. At every step I have to use my eyes together to make it work.

There is a stereoscope, a contraption with mirrors separating out two reflected images. I have to put the images together, get that chicken into the house! I do this for convergence at ever narrower angles, and then for divergence with angles spread out more and more. Each of these exercises is progressive—extremely hard at first, then easier as I get used to it. At first, coming out of the therapy each day, I feel demolished; it is very hard work for the brain as much as the eyes, and it affects the rest of my day. But as I get more used to things, I come to depend on it; no day feels complete unless I have done my therapy. Afterwards I feel lucid, clearer.

My favourite exercise is a lightboard, which I approach without my glasses on, visually naked, just myself and the lights. Here, as small bulbs flash on in front of me in random sequence, top, bottom, left and right in a grid, I must make instinctive leaps of the hand to switch them off. I feel I am my old soccer player, reflexes attuned, getting faster and faster, and what a revelation when I learn not to limit myself with tentativeness or thought. I get competitive, wanting to set a lightboard record for the office. Through it all, I learn to trust what I see, not hesitate about what I feel I ought to see, just be myself, let myself go.

But there are also moments of real pain when the memory embedded in my eyes comes to the surface, as almost literally I have to confront it. And so I learn what I have always suspected, that my physical system is connected with my mind and memory, my memory with body and mind. Here the revelation, difficult as it is sometimes, is to be working from body to mind rather than the other way round, which most of us are accustomed to doing. One day, using the stereoscope, I pull away in acute pain, I feel heat along the lower lid of my right eye, and discover that I am in tears. I can only feel that it is the pain of the knife when the surgeon made his cut and the left eye was horrified. It sounds like mystery and magic, but it is the truth.

Progressively, through doing the exercises, I learn what it has meant to me to be marked, and what it means to see the marking in a different way. It is like a personal archaeology in time, in space, in mind and body. To see is to be seen: I formulate this carefully. To be in a state of 'visibility'—being able to see—means being willing to be seen in the world. How strange that it is my eyes, the very instruments of my sight, that flinch from being seen. How has this affected their vision? Am I prepared to be free, to become 'visible'? I know what I know, but how will I confront it?

The child coming into the world does not know anything about being marked. Let the eyes go, let the tension behind them go, let the mind stop holding onto what it has come to see and be, how it expects to see, how it expects the self to be seen.

The barrier is the gateway to the path, and it is also the gateway to the past. The vision exercises become an exercise of my spirit, and in time I feel a liberation, lifting.

I look again at the circles. Present and past gaze at one another in the space of the mind. I am the barrier, I am the path. I am the present, I am the past. I and everything in that I. I/eye, eyes/I. In every sense this is a story not of a coming of age but of perspective.

There is another history under the one we readily see.

47 ⤚

FROM *The Vision Notebooks*

Across the years, an eye looking at an eye, looking at an I. Double vision: myself then, myself now, both in movement, parallax; the hologram builds up, dissipates. My birthmark becomes paler, lighter, and I am further away from home in both space and time. My vision therapy begins to rebalance what is out of joint, and it is disconcerting. Will there be marginal improvements, accommodations in the system that exists, or is the system itself the hindrance, so that I will have to let go of it entirely, see dislocated and blurred for a while before everything takes shape again? Will this be the equivalent of walking through the wall to find myself on the other side? If so, what will that other side be, and am I prepared to take the risk? What memories are buried in the way I see, what realities of the self that I will have to recognise? I am my own experiment, both subject and object of the investigation, seeing the self even as I am the self who is trying to see.

*

Don't look for any answers, because by definition you don't know what you are looking for, and also you don't know how to look.

*

I look at my eye in the mirror, see along the lid the deformations left by the operation, the unevenness like some planetary landscape. I look at everything as dispassionately as I can. The irregularities have caused my eyelashes to grow inward, and sometimes I am in agony, a stabbing pinprick direct to the surface from a sharp and sometimes invisible lash. Various doctors have tried to get these lashes out permanently, electrolyse or freeze them, but it has never worked. So every few weeks I pluck them out, not only those I can see but also the colourless ones I call albinos, which I have to find by intuition, habit and feel. I walk along a knife's edge (the metaphor not innocent in this case) with the tweezers, hoping my hand never slips. There is always irritation in my eye; the lubrication does not work because the tear ducts were harmed in the surgery. My eye is a sensitive gauge; as well as its state of alternating dryness and thick viscosity—its reflexes trying desperately to deal with whatever is in there, often stray eyelashes that simply fall in—at the slightest provocation it will simply weep copiously, whether in cold wind or emotional moments in films. It has become my inner barometer, the state of my being. It is my perpetual confession, who I am.

I am used to looking at the inner corner every day in the mirror, getting things out, using tweezers every few days, basic maintenance. These are the facts of what I do. But oh the relief when I get one of those eyelashes out that has been piercing me. What it means to breathe deeply again.

*

Wearing glasses has become my form of protection, a protective barrier between me and the world. Somehow, I imagine people can't see me through my lenses, particularly my right eye. But the lenses are there to help me see through, not to defend me. If Dr R talks of convergence—using both eyes to see together—I become aware of what I call 'aversion'. That is my version of things: looking away and down, not being willing to look others in the eye.

✻

I have got lost in the dark in the night, losing my normally sure-footed way, veering to the left, not knowing where I am, bumping into walls.

✻

In the exercises, things that appear to come towards me make me flinch, turn away. There is pain which I can feel, and sadness. I relive the moment of what I imagine is seeing the knife. But how can I know? Am I making it all up? I find the limit position of my vision, areas I will not look into and cannot see through. It is like the limit of consciousness, of sleep. A friend misquotes Wittgenstein to me, but nonetheless: 'I am sitting here but I don't believe it.' Yes, that is the feeling.

✻

But when there is release, letting go, the neck unlocks, the feeling of density behind my right eye dissolves. Astonishing sharp lucid clarity. Rich black ink against beautiful white space.

✻

My concerns are a study in method: how to see better using only damaged instruments to do so. Or to put it in a different way: the only instruments I can use are the very problem I am trying to fix. This means improving my eyes by seeing in a different way. Is that possible?

Effect alters cause: how difficult and how paradoxical! Can an improved vision of the world change the very form in which we see it, change who we are? And might that provide healing not only for ourselves but the world, help undo a history of damage? What would such a vision be like?

*

I have reinterpreted the recurring dream from my early years, of falling from the sky and dissolving as I am about to hit the ground. I regard it now as prophetic in the true sense. The 'I' is what must dissolve if I am to get through the barrier. And then it can reassemble, find itself, like coming out of water, waking from a dream.

*

For me, sadness is a state of being subdued, of being governed by the world. The body of repression must become the body of expression. Blake has a view on this: 'Rather murder an infant in its cradle than nurse unacted desires.' I don't want to go as far as murdering any infants, but I also don't feel like confining myself just to suit what I *imagine* the world wants of me. I have to get beyond that imagining. I must live in a body without adjectives.

*

When I do the exercises and everything releases, there is a lengthening around a curve, an arch in the back, a female version of pleasure. I feel more lithe, more feline, not the male dogsbody, mute.

*

Look to be liberated! Look—to be liberated ... Look, to be liberated.
The difference that punctuation makes; modalities in direction and
time.

*

I have been to see my aunt, my mother's eldest sister, whose mind to
me has always been a model of clarity. I mentioned that I had always
regarded her as a precise observer of people and things, but she said
that hadn't always been so. 'I learned to look in my late thirties,
early forties. It was at the time of my divorce. I felt like nothing, as
if people literally could not see me. So I began to look at people,
observe them, take an interest in them. And after a while I felt that I
was there too.'

*

I have had a conversation with Moira, in the open, next to the river,
things she knew already. Much is flowing, released.

*

How evasive is my honesty?

*

Look in the area of damage. Look through the blind spot. Overcome
the area of fear. The question is not whether I can see better. The
question is whether I can become the person who will see better.

201

*

Every image is a translation; there is no such thing as the literal. So we have the bodily metaphors: 'holding back'; 'vision'; 'blind spot'; 'aversion'; 'clarity'. These metaphors become physically embedded in the body and orientations of the mind.

*

I must change my fixation on my right eye. I do a thought experiment. The left eye has a birthmark as well. How does that feel? And then another experiment: *everyone* has a birthmark. How does *that* feel?

*

What do people do when they are in a place where nothing is clear? They must proceed by way of unknowing towards understanding.

*

There are moments of sudden breakthrough. It is almost like a shutter-shift in the eye, and things I couldn't see before come into view. The eye lets go of its attachment to the lid, there is an unclenching, lubrication. The birthmark is *under* the eye, it is not the eye, and I can feel the difference. But oh how I wish the original mark had not been damaged in that operation! That was the wound I still feel, still flinch from.

202

*

Acceptance, where I must go: 'This thing of darkness I acknowledge mine.'

*

My birthmark is not only my wound, it is my decoration. Can there be beauty as well in the darkness?

'Mascara', from the Italian, Catalan, Portuguese, meaning both 'mask' and 'stain'. A stain and a mask for beauty.

Not such a paradox after all. My-scar-eye, mascara. I smile in a different way.

⌒ 48

It is June 2002, and I am reading a sequence in a book which has
shaken me to the core. The book is W.G. Sebald's *Austerlitz*, an
account of a man who was taken out of Czechoslovakia as a child
on one of the *kindertransport* trains, but has lost all memory of it.
The book is without chapters, almost without paragraphs, and I had
nearly put it aside; it seemed almost monomaniacal in its pursuit
of Austerlitz's memories as relayed by a narrator who meets him in
various settings in Europe. But loving Sebald's other works, I stuck
with it, and gradually the book took over. And then the sequence
began. Austerlitz has retired to his home in the East End of London.
He tells the narrator how he had brought all his papers there to
work on his magnum opus, a study of European architecture. But
working in solitude, with scarcely any friends, there is crisis. He
finds he cannot write, even a sentence. Reading fails him, and then
even simple speech.

He takes to wandering the streets of London, all night long, night
after night. He seems a ghost in his own life, in the landscapes of the
dark. One evening he goes to Liverpool Street Station, and amidst
the vaults and gloom finds himself in the disused ladies' waiting
room. He steps inside, and there, in light falling in unreal curls and
patterns, he sees a man and a woman—the man in a dog collar, the
woman in 1930s dress. And there is also a boy sitting on a bench,
with knee-high socks and rucksack, waiting for them. The boy is
none other than himself. There he is, four years old, waiting to meet

the adoptive parents who took him off to live in fear and austerity in Wales, to lose his language, his name, his memories, which have been wholly suppressed until now. He has met himself in the station of memory: boy to man, man to boy, gazing at himself.

Some days later, Austerlitz is in a shop, and on the radio hears two women talking, remembering their childhood experience of being exiled on a *kindertransport*. One of them mentions the name 'Prague', and through a form of almost subconscious navigation, Austerlitz knows he must go there. In Prague he meets the woman who was friend to his mother and father, his own beloved nurse, with whom he had spoken in French and Czech as a child. 'Austerlitz, is that really you?' she says when she sees him. Now, though he had memorised some lines of Czech to ask his first questions, suddenly he can speak Czech again, the lost language.

I can't tell you how much these scenes rocked me, how the moment in the station waiting room felt completely uncanny, how it shivered me in awe and something like terror. All of it seemed to matter: Austerlitz's loss of language, the promptings of what he had forgotten, the unconscious maze he had to find his way through, the search for what was in his past, the encounter with the self he had completely lost, like a ghost in the waiting room of his life. I had no idea whether others would read the book in the same way as I did, but these scenes took me back instantly to my own waiting room of memory, as if the boy Austerlitz had seen was me, as if in this book I was reading something of my own life. As I read I returned to my own scene, of the operation on my eye when I was two, and some of Austerlitz's sadness descended upon me. I relived those moments in my own place of recognition. Here I imagined the nurse holding my hand; here I was as the knife came towards me to remove the mark of my identity forever. Here I was watching as if behind a window in the operating room; there I was on the table, seeing every moment and being unable to move or cry out, inside and outside myself at the same time. I knew what it was to see oneself, meet oneself in such a moment.

These scenes disturbed me for days, and they have never left me. In a way, I was able to feel through Austerlitz, a character who had lost the capacity to feel, a strange crossing from the book into life. Perhaps what I was feeling was not the pain of the original moment, but the shock of a moment in which recognition comes across the gaps of time and space and self. Of course there were differences. I was no Austerlitz; no trains lying in wait to take me to a different life—or death. I thought of my ancestors, what they had gone through because of their own marks of birth. I thought of South Africa, where I had been part of a system of demarcation and suffering. How to live with these moments of layered, simultaneous recognition! If one small event can so change a life, what is the sheer calculus of damage and loss in the world? Who can even begin to invent that mathematics?

For me then there was something about fate, and acceptance, and a commitment that suited who I was. Because I was marked, I was singled out and became marked again. This was my personal expulsion from Paradise, the angels' swords (or doctor's knife) above me, my second birth into the world, just as Adam and Eve were cast out. In the same way, many have been cast into the world beyond the gates where they must live out the consequences of their birthmarks.

See that child, see him growing through time, let him grow. Let him play soccer, let him read and play music, let him think. Find him in memory's waiting room and forgive him as he might forgive you. Accept the chasm not as the barrier to meaning but its precondition. Find that language. Dedicate yourself in the small acts of everyday to connection rather than division, for others as well as yourself. Understand that you see not despite the fact you are marked; it is the way you are marked that gives you your sight. Let it become your form of navigation, lead you towards a deeper vision.

49 ⌒

I have been reading Dr P's book, the man who did my operation. It
took some courage to read it, as for so long he has been a looming
mountain of a man for me, a monster shadow, a nemesis. Still,
I cannot allow him to become the complete bogeyman, and so I
pushed ahead page by page, keeping notes, half wondering whether
there might be any mention of a small boy and his birthmark. No
such luck, for I was not one of his successes, and this was a mostly
rambling account of the great doctor's triumphs. Those triumphs
were in their own way impressive: what would those burned airmen
have done without the possibility of reconstruction? And yet, I
discovered interesting things about the doctor. His book is entitled
The Right to Look Human, and for the umpteenth time I wonder
what being human looks like, especially in the charged racial
matrix of South Africa. He expatiates at length on how he works to
'improve' people's looks, but also says that if someone comes to him
wanting to look 'worse', he will refuse. Part of what improvement
means becomes clear when a woman comes to him to have her nostrils thinned so she will look less 'Coloured' and be able to marry
her white husband. This puts his eagerness to remove my 'black
mark', the blemish on white skin, in a different light. Perhaps it was
a project of 'improvement' along the same lines.

Indeed, through the course of the book I realise how far Dr

P's aesthetic philosophy was tied up with the racial hierarchies of apartheid. It also seems fitting that he became a brigadier in the South African Defence Force, going to Mozambique to report on the colonial war against the nationalist movement FRELIMO, where he writes of the fight against terrorism and communism in the exact language of the apartheid regime. At home, he says, we have to guard against moral degeneracy—leftist students, trade unionists, a permissive and dispirited youth. There is little here about the moral degeneracy of apartheid: not bad for a doctor concerned with 'the right to look human'.

*

Dream I. I was travelling to some new, foreign city, staying at a lavish hotel. It was night and we were in the ballroom area. A man and his daughter see me; he is well appointed. I see your birthmark, he says, and can fix it. It's so easy, these days there is no need to suffer. I have the ointment, a kind of liquid I'll apply. No, I say, people have tried, and I'm scared; you might burn me, harm me. No, he says, this is new. Then, I say, try it out on the beauty spot below my eye; if it works, we will do the rest. He puts it on and I go to sleep, and when I awake in the morning it's gone! My face feels fresh and new as if it has just been born. I can see and feel both sides of it. My eyes, looking out, are dark and luscious and clear. I look for the man so he can do the rest, but he is gone. Later in my half-dream before waking: it is my father. My body is shivering with emotion.

*

I have asked my mother about my operation, and she told me how it was. She told me how difficult it was for her and my father, how if she had known what was involved, she would never have let me

208

go. She told me that Dr P did use a knife to cut away, though he promised not to interfere with the eye. After it was over he told my parents he wanted to keep me, because I was so cute and alert. He reported that when I woke from the operation, I said I wanted something long and cold to drink. I also said, I have a headache, give me an aspirin. Later, at the age of six, when the birthmark had clearly come back and they took me to see him, he said, well, it's just the luck of the draw. After that my parents worried about me constantly in any new situation, but they took a decision not to shield or coddle me. I can only imagine how hard it must have been for them. How would I deal with it if it were a child of mine?

✻

How small my concerns are, though they have been big enough for me. Yet strange as the experience has been, I can't regret it. Perhaps in some parallel universe, on some other planet, I have been living a different life. But over here, on this one, this is the life I am living. If you asked me today whether, if the birthmark could suddenly disappear, I would take the option, I might be tempted, just to see what being unmarked is like. But there's also a good chance I would say no. Everyone is marked, and this is mine, and it has created the texture of my vision. Every mythic experience requires a visit to the underworld.

✻

Dream II. I was looking at some flowers, when suddenly two hummingbirds swooped by, one red, one green—the colours of the filters in the vision exercises. They were buzzing around my head, and instinctively I swatted them away, a gesture I instantly regretted. But they didn't leave. As they flew and swooped, I became dizzy with it, light-headed, intimations of a different state of being. And then the new state became me. I lifted off the ground like the hummingbirds, swirling around with them and then flying beyond them. I had accepted their dazzling colorations as my own. I had taken on their visibility, what I saw, and who I was.

✻

Breakthrough, doing my exercises. Centring above and behind both eyes, the body releases like a jolt of electricity, and I can see what I have not seen before. Out of the torque that has twisted my body there is energy and pleasure. I feel carnal in a boyish sort of way.

✻

What are daydreams? I can imagine they might provide a better route for therapy than dreams. I picture a therapist: 'Now daydream for me ...'

✻

I must change the grammar of how I see, the orientations of my inner language. I have identified myself so much with my right eye, it has seemed to be myself, who I am. But my conception must shift, so that I am in both eyes. I think of conflict in the world, South Africa, Palestine and Israel. People must be able to say, 'I am both sides, I can see through the eyes of both sides.' That is the only way forward. They have to see through and because of the damage; not the birthright but the birthmark which everyone has in different ways.

✻

In a kind of waking dream before dawn I was back in hospital, two years old. I felt the burning in the area under my eye, the burning of what had been done. I felt again—almost forced myself to feel—my parents gone from me, my radical bereftness and abandonment. Was I imagining this? I didn't know. I reached down, and from the depths of myself I allowed—I almost fetched it—a scream, a howl to emerge. I felt, this scream is public, and was amazed it didn't wake Moira. The howl was me, I was nothing more than the howl.

*

10 January 2003, the fifth anniversary of my father's death. I went to the synagogue to say Kaddish, surrounded by snow and cold, everything sparkling under the lights. I had a vision of him on the *koppie* where he is buried in Johannesburg, in the last hours of a warm summer night with the sky beginning to lift, dawn about to break, and the birds ready to burst into song.

*

One cannot postpone being. You cannot say, 'I'm not ready, I'll do it next week.'

*

I have been reading Freud's 'The Uncanny'—an eye-opening experience, so to speak. He writes of the connection between the *heimlich*—the secret—and the *heim*—the home. The secret is in the home, in what is most familiar. He writes that the fear of damaging or losing an eye is a terrible one in children; also that the fear of going blind is linked to castration. For no reason at all I think of the Cyclops, the one-eyed monster stabbed in the eye by Odysseus

211

and his comrades, who then escape by hiding under the woolly coverings of his sheep. If the one-eyed monster is the rampant male (a straightforward image in Freudian terms), then the covering is a female stratagem. Think of the Bible, how Rebecca won blind Isaac's blessing for Jacob and not Esau, disguising him in a covering of sheep's wool.

In a strange reversal my very own Cyclops, Dr P, tried to turn me into an image of himself, the one-eyed monster, knife to the eye when I had no defence. He tried to remove my covering, my stratagems, my laughter. From covering to recovering: seeing with both eyes, beyond monsters and heroes. I hope beyond knives and concealment.

✻

Freud also talks of 'the evil eye', a phrase that has always bothered me for obvious reasons. In German it is *der böse Blick*—the evil 'look'. The look: subjective and objective, how you see and how you appear. As ever, seeing is being seen, especially around questions of being marked as evil. We really do need a different vision, not to mention a new language.

✻

You cannot open the barrier by force; only by letting it go.

✻

16 April 2003. I graduated yesterday. I went in for my check-up, and Dr R pronounced me done. I was presented with a certificate, and a ring with an eye in it. All the helpers gathered round—Karen, Stephanie, Laura, Lori—like cheerleaders. I told them, today is the

212

day you can frame my credit card. I have to say that I was elated. It felt like an achievement, a memorable episode in my life, and though my journey with vision will continue, I felt no longer a student but a practitioner, licensed to 'be', so to speak. Dr R told me that when I first came to her, I had six units of vertical separation between my eyes. Even one unit, she said, is clinically significant. Now, though I wasn't wholly stable, she was not measuring any vertical separation. As for my horizontal resolution, I was firmly in the normal range.

I had an image of the small red inner-tube in the pool at the Oyster Box in Umhlanga Rocks, when I was learning to swim in that best, warmest, most amniotic water. It felt like I had been through a history, submerged, now breaking back to the surface in beautiful blue water and air, the conscious and subconscious, the dazzle of sea and sky, and living, breathing here.

✳

The Greek Dream. Last night's dream, the kind that says remember me. I was in Greece, first and most beloved place of my personal mythology. I was Greek, a ten-year-old boy, the age I was when the world was unbroken, when I walked in perfect balance in body and mind. The time felt classical or pre-classical; it was a city-state on cliffsides overlooking the sea. Water rushed over those cliffs, heading down vertically hundreds, even thousands of feet, crystal-clear water crashing down on rock platforms that jutted out and led into the sea. I was on top of a cliff that had at least two, maybe three sides, so that it was like a column rising out of the sea, joined on one side to the land. The custom in this society was for boys of a certain age, election and intention to undergo a rite of passage. They would stand on the edge of the cliff, their horses behind them, and then launch off in a forward dive, in the rushing water as they fell. Somehow they would gather themselves, their feet would come under them, they would land on one of the platforms and end swimming in the sea, their horses following after.

I was there, and for some reason felt no fear at all. I think my father was in the background; I had been dreaming about him all week. I stood on the edge of the cliff, water flowing all round, my horse behind me. There was a feeling that I should have chosen one of the other edges of the column with a wider platform into the sea below, but I had selected what I had selected or been selected by. That was where I was. So I collected myself and, eyes glistening, launched into the dive. I knew that somehow, magically, everyone or nearly everyone survived this; all I felt was a certain hesitancy about the height. The drop was straight down, except for some rocks protruding here and there.

So off I launch and down I go, and everything seems to be in slow motion. I feel I am not plummeting but swimming in air, because everything, including the water, is so clear. I can see rocks coming towards me, but with an innate ability that comes with the dive, I bring my feet under me, gather myself for a soft landing, and launch off from the rocks again in one motion. On one of these launches, as I lift out away again from the cliffside, my horse catches up with me, comes under me as I settle on his back, my very own Pegasus, and we are flying together as we land on the last platform and come to be swimming in the sea, from where we are brought in, greeted and welcomed.

Hologram

50 ⤳

When I arrived in England in October 1977 there was a heat wave, and I was sweltering in the winter clothes I had brought for the trip. After a day or so in London I made my way to Oxford by train, and then to my college, which I had applied to mainly because one of my university teachers in Johannesburg had gone there. I was carrying two suitcases, but they were so heavy that the handle of one of them broke. In the porter's lodge they told me I would be staying in a house the college owned in Manor Road some distance away, and asked if I wanted a 'truck' for my luggage. To me a truck was a lorry, like the Bedfords we had driven in the army, and it seemed a little excessive; only later did I discover that it meant a hand-cart, which would certainly have come in handy.

So I staggered off down High Street and Longwall to Manor Road, where I met my future companions for the year. There was Salman, elegant and patrician, whose grandfather had been the third president of India; I told him one of my Hebrew names was Zalman—a connection already! Rudra also came from India, but he was a Marxist, whereas Salman followed Indira Gandhi. There was Januscz, of Polish extraction from London, a mathematician who seemed to do most of his work lying down in thought on his bed and finished his doctorate before any of us. Next door were Mark, from America, and Alan, a Glaswegian philosopher who could drink like a wonder and, when he was involved in an argument, would turn up his accent by about fifteen degrees just to throw you off balance. When I arrived there was another Scot living on cornflake sandwiches, because his student grant had not yet come in.

There were others as well: Big Steve, an anthropologist (I was known as Little Steve, and then later Red Steve); there was a Scots sailor named Dusty who really was a Red, and who instituted an annual Robbie Burns Night in the college, where whisky was the only antidote to the haggis and vice versa; there was an Englishman, studying law, who in the evening would don a silk robe and slippers. Salman taught me the basics of Indian cooking; Rudra spoke passionately about the Indian Mutiny of 1857, though of course he didn't see it as a mutiny but rather an uprising with many local inflections; Mark became my very good friend, and later a clerk to Justice Blackmun in the US Supreme Court. The following year others arrived. James, from Australia, walked into the college with a copy of Dante in his back pocket which he was using to learn Italian, and then went on to win Oxford's Dante Prize. Amitav, also Indian, went off to Egypt for his research and came back to lock himself in a room and write the fastest thesis ever in Anthropology in Oxford, turning quite green in the process. One evening at a party he asked me if I had read the new novel by someone called Salman Rushdie; it gave him an idea, he said, of what could be done—and then he went off to become a famous novelist himself. Not all were so successful. A student called Dave went to somewhere like Indonesia, having devoted himself to the purity of anthropological investigation. But when the inhabitants of his remote village asked him for a tape recorder before they would speak to him 'because the previous anthropologist gave us one', we heard he had something of a breakdown.

When I was applying for admission to Oxford I had made a conscious decision not to enter for the Rhodes Scholarship because it was still a segregated award, not open to black South Africans. So I put my name in the general pool, administered by the university, and they gave me a scholarship for Jewish students, which seemed to defeat the point just a bit. Once I arrived in England, it took me months to settle down, my nerves jangled from the experience of the previous years. As we walked two-by-two wearing half-length black gowns towards the Sheldonian Theatre to 'matriculate'—formally enter the university—I experienced a familiar other-planetary sensation, for I had come from a war zone. When I went into a left-wing bookstore in London, scanning the shelves for all the titles banned in South Africa, I looked over my shoulders to see who was there, out of habit and because London—we were told—was full of spies. In Oxford, if I saw a policeman walking towards me, I would cross the road to the other side. Taxis in Oxford had blue lights on their roofs much like police cars in South Africa, and if one of them raced up my heart would start pounding. How different was my friend Mark, with his New York habits. He would ride his bicycle at night without a light the wrong way down Carfax, and get mightily offended when a policeman stopped him. He would bang on the doors of passing cars if they came too close to him crossing the road.

At the end of my first year when Moira was coming to join me, I had to make arrangements for our wedding. One task was to find a venue for the reception, and at first I thought of our college cemetery; it dated back to the fourteenth century or so, and as summer approached the students would suntan on the gravestones. I had become quite used to it, but then it dawned on me that a wedding celebration in a cemetery might not mark the most auspicious beginning. I went back and forth to London answering detailed questions about family lineage so that we could get a rabbi for the ceremony. Then Moira arrived, we saw Bob Dylan and got stuck in the Reading station waiting room, and Mark, who was to be my best man, arranged a wine-tasting event for our reception that went on for about two and a half days. After we were married we went to Greece, and one evening, across from the Acropolis, followed the sounds of a guitar and a beautiful voice until they led us to a restaurant in a garden. We had very little money, but the waiter brought us food for what we could afford, and thereafter, as a gift from the owner, the most wonderful dessert wine from the island of Samos. It was a quite magical evening, and it inspired us, by means of an execrably long ferry ride, to go to Samos itself, almost within sight of Turkey. There, along with the bright waters and beautiful beaches, we found the beginnings of a new German invasion— of tourists. For someone such as myself, who went through life expecting the Third Panzer Division to burst out of the forests at any moment, it was unnerving. Still, we rode on small motorbikes around the island, and in one town square saw a dysmorphic statue of a lion sculpted by someone who clearly had never seen one.

When we flew back to England on a charter plane that alarmingly leaked liquid down its inside walls all the way we didn't know how married people behaved at passport control, and so went to different counters. There Moira was threatened with immediate deportation because the officer thought she had married a British citizen in order to stay in the country. Hearing the commotion, I came over, and explained that I was also South African. It took a while to sort out, and we had to go to the immigration authorities in the aptly named Lunar House in London to do so. Not for the first or last time in Europe we found ourselves among all the suspect and unwanted—we because we carried South African passports, the others invariably because they were black or came from third world countries. In Oxford every year we had to report to the police station to update our documents. There, when the phone rang, a very kindly sergeant would pick it up pleasantly and announce, 'Hello, Aliens.'

If I had any guiding idea by the time I left Johannesburg it was that of metaphor. With a little Vico behind me, I fashioned the idea that all histories were metaphoric equivalents; the facts might change through time, but the patterns of experience, and their relative intensity, remained more or less constant. Unschooled, I was making things up, but this particular idea was perhaps a way of coping with the brutality of the history we were facing, a consolation and also an escape. When I first arrived in Oxford I attended a packed lecture by the rising Marxist critic Terry Eagleton. At one point he asked what the essential nature of literature was (meaning of course to show there was no such thing). After a number of answers had been offered, I summoned up my courage at the back of the hall and said it was metaphoric. Well, said Eagleton, couldn't it be metonymic as well? Why yes, of course it could, I said, and sat down hurriedly, not knowing what on earth metonymy really was (it took me years to work out its intricacies). Some months later, Mark and I were on a hiking trip in Wales, and had a voluble argument about the existence of God in a pub, while the locals looked on in disbelief. To me, as I argued, it seemed that if one had a powerful inner sensation of God's existence, it was all the proof that was required. It was like a particular sensory organ for the purpose, and similar to the way one trusted vision, if more ethereal; you didn't doubt the things you were seeing.

But history and metaphor, the seen and unseen, seemed to be finding their own way towards one another. When I left South Africa, one of the professors who ran the English department had told me I was heading for trouble in Oxford, saying I was too big for my boots, that my writing was terrible, that if I wanted a model to aspire to—he looked up at the ceiling as he said this—well, he could think of no one better than John Bayley. John Bayley was something else I hadn't heard of, but my path led with a certain inevitability towards him. Trying to understand how history was embedded in fiction, I started reading African literature, then South African literature (which we had never studied in Johannesburg), and afterwards I found my way to Nadine Gordimer. The Oxford English faculty, in its wisdom, handed me to John Bayley, the only person prepared to take on every outlandish topic. When I wrote my first piece for him, I came to his rooms in some anxiety, expecting the worst as had been prophesied. But when I had picked my way through the papers littering every inch of the floor and found a place to sit, Professor Bayley found my essay and looked up. Then, with his engaging stammer he said, 'Y-you know, I qui-quite enjoyed this.' I discovered later it was one of his highest forms of praise.

John Bayley was perhaps the classic liberal literary critic, whereas I was now tending more towards Eagleton's radical approach. But, like a good liberal, Bayley had an essential tolerance for what I was doing, and I learned an openness from him that never left me. Sometimes he and his wife, the venerable novelist Iris Murdoch, would come over for dinner, bringing their own wine, uncorked, so they would not have to contemplate whatever undrinkable substance graduate students might provide. Once, as summer approached, Bayley invited us to their house in the village of Steeple Aston. As we had a car by then—a Citroën Deux Chevaux, right-hand drive and almost no power (it was good for a conversation, said the person who sold it to us, but even that wasn't true because of the noise)—he asked if we could bring over another couple, an American student and his wife. Duly, we picked them up, and all the way to Steeple Aston the Americans were agog at the idea of being alone with John and Iris, talking over a glass of sherry or wine. We arrived to find cars parked all the way down the road; this was our hosts' way of discharging all their social obligations at once. The Americans were disconsolate, but we had fun nonetheless in the Bayley-Murdoch garden, overgrown as it was with grass and weeds, and I diverted myself talking with a Hungarian philosopher who said he had been working for the last twenty years on the concept of time.

Finally it was time to leave; in the English way, people were beginning to go, and we knew the signals. Oh no, said the Americans, can't we stay just a bit, you know to chat with John and Iris, have a glass of wine or sherry? I said, one more walk around the garden and then we are leaving. When Moira and I got back, the place was deserted, John and Iris nowhere to be seen, and so the four of us tiptoed our way out through the house. That is, until the Americans saw the debris of the party, and felt in their earnest way that we had to help clean up. I demurred, knowing something about English privacy, and in any case Moira and I had no inclination to deal with such a vast mess. So we made ourselves scarce while the Americans ferried things back and forward to the kitchen. At that point, Iris Murdoch entered the room like something blown in by a hurricane. 'Thank you,' she said in a voice which made the word 'imperious' seem feeble by comparison, 'that will be quite enough!' And before we knew it, we had been ushered with a firm smile towards the front door, which then slammed shut behind us with unmistakable finality. We made our way sheepishly towards the car—we only wanted to help, lamented the Americans—but just then John Bayley came tripping down the road in his elf-like way. 'Oh,' he said, 'are-are you l-leaving s-so soon? Why not c-come b-back for a g-glass of w-wine? Iris will be *s-so* pleased!'

So it was through an unexpected combination of John Bayley and Terry Eagleton, as well as a group of South African historians into whose orbit I had been generously welcomed, that some time later I came to be standing outside a wooden door to a garden in Johannesburg at eight o'clock in the morning, waiting in trepidation to meet Nadine Gordimer. She had a fierce reputation, but was more than kind to me, prepared to talk at length and answer my questions. She asked if I was interested in her manuscripts and papers, unsorted and uncollected upstairs in a tin trunk and cabinet, and of course I said yes. There I found some of her earliest writings, of her travels to Egypt, the Congo, Madagascar and elsewhere, as well as an early unfinished novel. There was a copy of *Playboy* magazine, where an excerpt from her novel *The Conservationist* had been published, and one of *London Magazine* with a photograph of Allen Ginsberg and a couple of friends naked, all banned materials in South Africa. Later she showed me a copy of the *African Communist*, journal of the South African Communist Party, published in a special, small, struggle-size version, containing a spiteful review of her novel *Burger's Daughter*, delivered purposely and secretly to her door.

The arc of the pendulum had taken me away but had brought me back again. Normally the swing of a pendulum lessens over time until it is still, but mine has only increased, moving further and further away. Yet the parabola, almost invisible now, remains. Contrary to the standard laws of physics, you can be in two places at once, like electrons travelling in different directions which remain entangled in their spin and movement, connected in their behaviour. Across space, across time, the arc suggests a map not easily captured by most of the known forms of cartography. It is a map of invisible links, invisible inks, uncanny hauntings and double vision, and who knows by what compass or stars we really navigate.

51

It was April 1994, and we were living in Washington DC, where I had a fellowship at the Woodrow Wilson Center for the year. My office was up one of the turrets in the Smithsonian headquarters on the Mall, in a building known, because of its features, as the Castle. Looking out of my window to the left was the Natural History Museum, straight ahead the National Air and Space Museum and the Capitol. I was at the centre of power in the world, probably in the known universe. Certainly some of the fellows behaved as if it was. There was one, an expert on foreign and military policy I came to think of as Dr Death; among other things he volunteered that he never read books any more but 'broke their spines' in order to scan them. In my mind I concocted a Smithsonian murder mystery in which he was found dead at his desk early one morning, and absolutely everyone had a motive.

Washington DC was also a heavily segregated city. We had seen this before when we lived in New Haven for a year, on a borderline street where (someone suggested) more people came in your front window than your front door. But Washington was much worse. Just behind the Capitol building were black areas where poverty ruled and violent death was a fact of life; it felt more than a little like Johannesburg. I came to learn more about it by talking with one of the cleaners in our building, a man named Michael, something of a black nationalist who at first wanted nothing to do with me because I was a white South African. But in time we had long conversations:

I was working on a biography of a white man who had worked closely with Nelson Mandela. We had a lot to discuss. By the time I left, Michael wanted me to go on a local radio station for a talk show with one of his nationalist friends, but politely I turned him down: conversation was one thing, target practice in which I would very likely be the target was another.

This day in April 1994 was not just any day. It was 26 April, the day voting opened for those living overseas in South Africa's first free and democratic election. Over the next few days, people queued up before dawn in South Africa to vote, and aerial pictures showed lines snaking for what seemed like miles around the polling stations. Information in Washington DC had been confusing, but we understood that we would be allowed to participate, though we had lived outside the country for some years. Our South African passports would be our identification. Moira and I made our way to the South African embassy, filled with a sense of anticipation and reverence. Neither of us had ever voted before, not even in South Africa when we had been entitled to. This was partly because we had refused to participate in apartheid elections; but also because there was no one to vote for in our constituencies who represented anything like our views. So this would be the first time for us as for millions of others.

When we arrived at the embassy, the atmosphere was mixed—decorous and solemn, but also demotic and ordinary. People arrived with a certain look in their eyes, not talking much, and there to meet us was a white woman whose mail order company, catering to the nostalgia for South African goods, had helped provide lists of expatriates to the embassy. She was if anything a *kugel* of the classic Johannesburg type, with a nasal voice and heavy make-up. We joined the line, snaking in this instance only around the room, blacks and whites together. Our fingers were marked with purple ink to register the fact that we were voting, and though we had our passports, we found to our surprise that proof of citizenship did not matter. It seemed emblematic of the day that because of the difficult journeys many had been forced to take, the simple claim of citizenship at any stage of one's life was sufficient. We received our ballots, and I marked mine for the ANC, next to the picture of Nelson Mandela. As I dropped the ballot into the box, I was aware of the significance of the moment—or at least I tried hard to be. I thought of the simultaneity, offset by hours around the globe, as millions of South Africans would be casting their votes, entering a new world. I thought of the generations who were not there to see the election, and those who had been imprisoned to make it happen. I thought of Bram Fischer, whose life I was writing, and what it might have meant to him. In short, I tried to invest every microsecond of the time it took to deposit the ballot with a full sense of its presence and meaning, to record it in my mind forever. Even as I did so it slipped away; I was trying too hard, aware also of how my own feeling could not measure up to the moment. But underneath was a substratum: a sensation which I did not even think of suppressing, of simple, unmitigated joy.

I imagine I must have thought back, during the course of the day, to the time I had met Nelson Mandela to interview him about Bram Fischer. Fischer had been born in 1908 into a distinguished Afrikaner nationalist family, and such were his magnetism and talents that he was expected to become either prime minister or chief justice of South Africa. Yet in the 1930s—he was a Rhodes Scholar, he travelled in Europe and saw the rise of Nazism, he travelled to the Soviet Union—he came to identify with the majority of South Africa's people. Never abandoning his Afrikaner identity, he became a communist, working with all the leading political lights of the time. Not least, he was tremendously important as an advocate, active in all the major political trials. He helped win acquittal for all 156 accused in the Treason Trial of 1956–61. In 1964, at great risk to himself, he led Nelson Mandela's defence at the Rivonia Trial, helping to save Mandela's life and ensuring—though he could not have known it at the time—that Mandela would emerge from prison some twenty-six years later to introduce South Africa's peaceful revolution. During that trial Fischer had seen documents handed into court that were in his own handwriting; he could just as easily have been among the accused. In 1965, after going underground and spending more than nine months in disguise—a distinguished advocate no less—he himself was captured and sentenced to life imprisonment. He was released (though still in the status of a prisoner) only when he was dying of cancer in 1975, and after his cremation his ashes were retained by the South African state as property of the Prisons Department. The Afrikaners of that time could not forgive him his treason towards his people, though of course he did not see it that way.

It was in this context that I came to meet Nelson Mandela in December 1991. The negotiations which would settle the future dispensation of South Africa were fully under way, but it was also a time of virtually apocalyptic chaos as various parties and constituencies jockeyed for ascendancy with unrestrained violence. Every day brought notice of new threats and outrages. On the extreme right the racist Afrikaner Weerstandsbeweging led by Eugène Terre'Blanche staged rallies and attacks flaunting its quasi-Nazi insignia. In one of the more confusing symptoms of the time Chief Mangosuthu Buthelezi's Inkatha movement, fashioning itself in opposition to Mandela's ANC, seemed to be in alliance with the shadier forces of the South African state. Hostel-dwellers, the main source of Inkatha support in the urban areas of Johannesburg, undertook horrendous attacks on students and community members. And then there were the occult organs of the state itself—the so-called Third Force, neither police nor army, yet incorporating elements of both, whose main purpose appeared to be mayhem, disruption and death.

228

Now the negotiations were in abeyance for a while—there was a short break at the end of the year—and it allowed just the slimmest opportunity to reach Mr Mandela, who was taking a few days' respite. My approach went through friends and associates in the legal world, in particular Arthur Chaskalson and George Bizos, who as young advocates had been part of the Rivonia defence team. Eventually, word came via George one Friday that I should be ready to meet Mr Mandela that evening. I was due to go out, but of course those plans changed. And then came a further message: he wanted me to come on the Saturday morning instead. Nelson Mandela wanted to take the time to think about Bram Fischer.

On the Saturday morning, George came to fetch me in his Mercedes-Benz. We were to go to a certain flat in Yeoville where we would be given further instructions, for Mandela's location was secret. At the flat we were met by his minders, two young ANC security men; and Barbara Masekela, sister of the trumpeter Hugh Masekela and later ambassador to the United States, also wandered through. The two minders instructed us to follow them by car across Johannesburg, and eventually we came to a northern suburbs mansion which had been loaned to Mandela as a retreat while the negotiations were on hold. We drove in, parked, and were shown to the living room, where we waited. Finally, Nelson Mandela emerged from the interior of the house. Tall and angular, he was wearing a blue tracksuit with a metallic sheen, and he greeted George effusively; they were old friends. All I had with me was a rather battered tape recorder, and sitting across from Mr Mandela, I opened nervously, but he stopped me. Before I asked questions, he said, there were things he wanted to tell me about Bram Fischer. And then, with a somewhat old-worldly air, he began a short speech in which I could see the structure he must have mapped out the previous evening: point 1, point 2, subsection a, b, c. It was clear that he really had taken the time to think, and other aspects impressed me no less. He spoke of how, when he was starting out in the ANC, he had wanted nothing to do with members of other races, how communism had seemed just one more foreign ideology. Yet the presence of individuals such as Bram Fischer, Yusuf Dadoo and others had shown him that people across the spectrum were prepared to take the same risks as black South Africans and had a role to play. Concerning his earlier phase, I asked him what, if anything, he and his comrades had expected whites in the Communist Party to do, since by definition they could not join the ANC. His response was intriguing: 'Well, I don't think we ever considered that question, and even as you put it, I find it difficult to face.' Unlike most politicians, he was prepared to think seriously about questions and answer them honestly; but then he wasn't simply a politician.

I left that day thinking that if Nelson Mandela asked me to do just about anything, I almost certainly would. Such was his command, his demeanour, his stature. I had experienced a related but different sensation some three weeks earlier when I went to interview his long-time comrade Walter Sisulu. I met Sisulu in an office block in the city centre in Johannesburg that the ANC had taken as its headquarters. After I had gone through security (my briefcase, carrying my recorder, beeped, at which the guards passed the case around the metal detector and let me through—so much for security), I found Sisulu, a small and somewhat rotund man, sitting at a desk in the middle of an enormous office, looking stranded and out of place. But as soon as we spoke, I was completely won over by his warmth and humanity. He told me how, when he would stay at Bram Fischer's house in the 1950s, he would hear Bram going to his son Paul's room when Paul would cough in the night. Paul had cystic fibrosis, and died at the age of twenty-three; Bram, in prison, was not allowed to attend the funeral. The Fischers felt like family, said Sisulu, and when he heard that Paul was gone, 'it was as if my own son had died'. I realised then how much South Africa had depended on personal relationships for the non-racial vision that would guide us, how much on a remarkable set of individuals. No matter what happened in South Africa, no subsequent history could change that. By the time I left Sisulu, I felt that if he too asked me to do just about anything, I almost certainly would. But whereas with Mandela it would have been out of awe, for Sisulu it would have been out of love.

⌐ 52

Living in America.
   'Are you all together?'
   'Today we are.'
   Jazz forms in the park.

It was December 2001, and I had arrived in New Orleans the night before, reluctantly, to attend a conference. September 11th had come and gone, and I didn't feel like travelling. But there I was, in the city of New Orleans, and on that first morning, turning my back on the conference, I decided to head out. I made my way down into the French Quarter, itself just beginning to wake up. The place looked a bit bleached, and some storefront sidewalks were being washed after what must have been a strenuous night. Yet the atmosphere of those low buildings, their wrought-iron balustrades and intimacy with the streets, was unmistakable. Even in the too-early morning, in air surprisingly sharp and cold, my jaded feeling began to lift in a sense of strange enchantment.

I found myself in Jackson Square, with its multiple legacies, Spanish and French, and sought out a bench in the sun. I was in a park of sorts, facing aslant a monument of General Jackson on his horse, when I heard, first, an accordionist, playing in one corner of the square, Cajun-style. Then, behind me, a mouth organ, a rampant blues. They were playing separately, and it was a few minutes before I realised how their sounds were wafting, flowing through one another. If you listened to them together, it was jazz; the city beginning to make its music. When I wandered across to look, I saw the accordionist playing her instrument in a kind of loping dance, as if possessed by the music she was making. Yet she also smiled at a small child she was playing for.

Then flowing through it was other music, this time what sounded like a jazz ensemble. A band was beginning to form, facing the easy steps of the Cabildo, and I went over to see. The guitarist was the only one sitting down, playing slick acoustic rhythms on a bench. Behind him and to the side were two trombonists and a horn player. There was a cardboard box in front, for money. To begin with the crowd was slow, but soon things began to warm up. They played swing, and blues, and songs with the mournful, joyous sounds only a New Orleans band can make: 'I went down to St James infirmary'.

New musicians arrived to join the group; one by one they seemed to appear out of nowhere. If you happened to look away, sure enough when you turned back there was someone else playing. A tuba player joined, his instrument wrapped copiously with duct tape. The guitarist was the youngest, and the only white musician; he played with half-gloved fingers because of the cold, a cloth cap on his head and a beatific smile. Then an old man arrived, playing bass—superb bass. He wore heavy work-boots, blue jeans with three-inch turn-ups, a sweater with a hood to cover his head, and a second covering with another hood over that. He was unshaven, and bent over almost double as he leaned across the bass, so that you might think he could barely stand up; but his fingers walked up and down the fingerboard as if out for the most ready of saunters.

Then a washboard player arrived. And a female clarinettist, who laid her head back and played dazzling runs to the skies as if the devil were in her feet and God just a few yards above her head. And they played the crowd, laughing, cajoling, interjecting, hustling. The crowd grew and grew, and so did the money in the box—which after a while became a bucket—as they walked it around. Meanwhile, through it all the horn player chainsmoked. He played his solos head down into his instrument, working with one hand only, cigarette dangling smoke in the other. The trombonist belted out the vocals just like a Louis Armstrong, and even managed to look like him. This, I felt, was how Armstrong might have sounded on the streets, with that extraordinary combination of beaming charm, smile, hustle and survival. I had known something about all this before, but now it was as if a shutter had shifted almost physically in my mind. There was a story written there that set the American picture in a different light.

I left once, but had to come back, to hear more. The sun was fully up in the sky, the atmosphere one of joy and celebration; there must have been a crowd of five hundred, transported in the moment they were part of. As for me, I felt simply exhilarated.

Before I left the first time, the clarinettist came by with the bucket, to collect money, and also to sell her CDs. It was then that I asked her: 'Are you all together?' Though I had said it awkwardly, I had meant, are you a band, do you always play with one another?

There was a glint in her eyes as she took some time considering the question in all its ramifications: 'Today we are,' she said.

*

I had never really wanted to come to the United States.

When I was a child, along with all my friends I read American comics: Archie and Jughead, Sad Sack, Casper the Friendly Ghost, and the others. On the back pages were adverts for Americana unavailable to us in South Africa: BB guns, Schwinn bikes (crossbars shaped like futuristic rocketships), sneakers. The sneakers looked good, but it all seemed to belong to a different life form. Instead, if I thought of going anywhere, it was most likely to Australia, with its romance of cricket and the outback. Later, as I came to political and cultural consciousness, America was the Empire: overweening and daunting, a profoundly ambiguous country sometimes dangerous to herself and to others. I remember the shock when, with an almost concrete sense of chronology, I realised that Martin Luther King's march on Selma had occurred *after* the Sharpeville massacre in South Africa. I knew how bad *we* were: that was a given. But what remained to be done in America?

And here I was in America through a series of choices and accidents, trying to make sense of it all. In South Africa I had come to terms with a number of realities: my own marginality (understanding too how that can be a positive thing); the problem of vision in a distorted society so that every perspective has to be measured and measured again, from every angle. And yet there was the sheer intensity of that world, so that whole lifetimes could be lived in a day, always seeking out again and again an understanding of one's existence. Since I had left, we had had Nelson Mandela (my own vote in 1994, standing in line in Washington DC). And what did America have? Here I was, back in the belly of power, with an old and recognisable feeling. Perhaps dissidence is the only country of the honest, I had thought to myself in the plane on the way to the conference.

And yet, this glimpse of *another* America. How much history, in all its ambiguity and anguish, joy and complexity, was contained in the smile of a Louis Armstrong? How much was there in the music? Here, in the winter of New Orleans, it spoke to me of something, and of many things at once: of links across the globe; of endurance and what it takes to survive; of improvisation in all its manifold forms; of wit, intelligence and understanding. Understanding of myself too, in that moment, and across my own history.

✳

I walked into a store which I think was called Black Arts, drawn by black-and-white photos of the jazz greats in the window: Billie Holiday, John Coltrane, Dexter Gordon. At least, I tried to walk in, but couldn't get the door open. I thought it was locked, but a young African American woman working inside came and opened it for me. 'It just needs a push,' she said.

I looked at the posters, saw which I liked, and said I might come back on the Saturday to get one or more of them. The store also had paintings and drawings in other iconic formats—the sensuality of Josephine Baker, images overly sultry and exotic. But it was the jazz black-and-whites that took my fancy.

The young woman and I spoke a bit, inconsequentialities about New Orleans and its streets, the weather. Then I left, or tried to leave. Inside the store I had my bifocals on, dividing my vision near and far. They were new, and I was still getting used to them, feeling awkward. I pushed at the door, but again it wouldn't move. Then I realised, and pulled, and it opened.

I turned to look at the young woman, gazing at me with amusement—this intellectual who likes jazz and makes large pronouncements and can't open a door—but also with friendship and, I guessed, warmth.

'It opens inwards,' she mouthed through the glass.

53 ⌒

It was February 1998, and I was flying home to South Africa for the publication of my biography of Bram Fischer. The book had taken me an enormously long time—it was about as old as our daughter Amelia, soon to turn fourteen. There were to be special events in Johannesburg and Cape Town, and I would be able to see my parents as well, an important consideration as my mother had been ill. My parents had followed journeys of their own. They had lived in England for a while, where my father was cheated out of just about everything he possessed by a fraudulent company for which he worked. He had also given up his South African pensions to pay for his mother's care. And so they returned home to begin again, facing a future of decidedly uncertain prospects. My father abandoned his pride, and went to work again, first for a patent lawyer, then as a business officer in a ceramics factory, virtually anything he could turn his hand to. Where many of his contemporaries were retired, enjoying the ease of Johannesburg life yet complaining about conditions under the new South African dispensation, he was setting about his work without demur and becoming, if anything, increasingly radical in his views. My mother and father's customary generosity towards others was supplemented by a new fortitude and courage in their personal lives which you could only admire, but I also knew something had broken when I would ask my father how he was and he had taken to saying quietly, in the English way,

'Mustn't grumble.' My father didn't speak about things; you had to divine what he was feeling.

This was to be a journey of strange concatenations. For one thing, the reason I was travelling now was that the launch of the book was timed to coincide with the Bram Fischer Memorial Lecture, to be given by the chief justice of South Africa in the Parliament buildings in Cape Town. The lecture had been post-poned from the previous year, and the book had been delayed in production, but now the convergence seemed perfect. Yet in the weeks leading up to my flight, I had been virtually certain I would not get there. First I had an ear infection, no serious matter. But then had come chest pains—fierce pains, especially in the night, so I could hardly breathe. I didn't say a word to anyone, least of all a doctor, because I desperately wanted to make the trip and didn't want anyone to prevent me. But I feared for my health, and had the feeling I might never make that lecture in Parliament. In my office at work I wrote out a will, asked a secretary to witness it, and secreted it in my desk.

When I arrived at the airport in Johannesburg, they met me, my father white-haired and strained, but with a fierce, almost luminous intensity about him. My mother looked gaunt, and it shocked me, for I had never seen her quite like this. Retrieving the car from the parking lot, my father was full of his usual irascible aggravations as other drivers cut in, or he had to wait heading out at the kiosk to pay. And then he drove! Fast as always, if not faster. He had always been a superb driver with impeccable reflexes and instincts, but he was getting older, and there we were in the outside lane travelling at over 120 kilometres per hour. Anxious for my nephew and niece sitting on either side of me, I took the only tack I knew would work, and reminded him that in the middle seat at the back I had no seatbelt. He slowed down, suddenly realising, just a little, the state he was in. My brother and his wife were following, in their car.

*

That was on the Sunday, and over the next two days it was all I could do to get my father to slow down, to ease up. Since my mother had been ill, he had taken everything on himself—the flat, the shopping, and he was still working in the mornings. That of course left her without any control in her own life, and as always she felt his domination, his colonising tendencies. So they niggled at each other, verged on losing their tempers, but what really spoke through everything was the difficulty of their circumstances, their fears for the future, the sheer stress of their lives as they now knew them. On the Monday morning my father went to work, and we spent the afternoon absorbing and trying to get around the various tensions. He went into work again on the Tuesday, insisting that he would be back to take me to the bank to get some cash before I left for Cape Town in the afternoon. But when he returned from work, I saw how he was and said, 'Dad, forget about the bank. It will be fine. Let's just spend the time together.' Surprisingly, he relented, and so we stayed in the flat. I put on a tape of Amelia playing the violin, and he, my mother and I all listened together. For him it must have been special. Amelia was his kind of girl. He used to tease her, she would sparkle, they loved being together.

Then we left for the airport. There I offered to buy them something to eat and drink; they refused all but coffee and tea, the smallest things.

*

On the flight down to Cape Town I sat next to a young black man named Victor who had once been a literature student and knew some of my work. Now, however, he was in business and doing very well. He was not looking forward to being in Cape Town, calling it

239

'socially regressive'. He was also frank about the benefits of black empowerment, the new government policy. The world was full of opportunities for those who had never had any, he said. Yet he also shared some of the feelings about the crime and violence that threatened everyone in Johannesburg, where truly horrendous things occurred almost daily. In that way, Victor was now part of the white world; others did not worry so much. 'It's only the ones like me, who have moved to Sandton, who are anxious and fearful,' he said.

In Cape Town I was staying at my friend Stephen Watson's house. Over the high wall, at the back of his narrow garden in Rondebosch, rose the extraordinary silhouette of Table Mountain, mythic and transcendent yet at the same time strangely close and intimate. I slept out there, in a small cottage separate from the house, and right through the night my chest pains pounded again, except now it was worse. My chest was heaving and beating, my temples were throbbing, the pain was so excruciating that I felt I would not survive. I think I focused on staying awake as a way of holding onto life. Yet the morning came, and I was still there; so, feeling exhausted and unsettled, I headed off to be interviewed on my book. There was a radio conversation, and then another, most engaging, with a journalist from the *Cape Times* who, like Bram Fischer, was from the Orange Free State, and like me also had a birthmark on his face, though not of the same type. I remember walking uphill from one place to another with the publicist who was shepherding me around, concentrating on going slowly and breathing deeply so as not to provoke the pain in my chest.

I had a meeting lined up that afternoon at the university, to be followed by the memorial lecture, so I returned to Stephen's to change. There as I walked in the door, he came to meet me, saying my brother had phoned from Johannesburg, that it was urgent, and that I should call home immediately. It could only be my mother, I thought, as I phoned Paul, given that she had been so ill. But when he picked up the phone and spoke to me, he told me that my father had died. He had gone out to the shops and had collapsed, and was dead by the time the ambulance came.

It was one of those moments when reality seems quite unreal. It wasn't my mother, it was my father, he who was such a strong physical presence, the fast driver, with his lightning-quick responses. Now he was somehow no longer there. My first thought was: he waited for me to come. My second: thank God I was able to be here.

Paul said I should stay for the lecture if I wanted to, but naturally I decided to return home. Stephen helped me change my flight, and while I was waiting to leave, a colleague and friend, Nick Visser, came to visit. Nick was suffering from pancreatic cancer, and had made a decision not to take any treatment but to live out his life in awareness and dignity for as long as it lasted. There in the garden at Stephen Watson's, a dying man consoled one whose father had just died. Fifteen years later, Stephen also died from cancer, loss resonating with loss.

*

My father said to me once, 'It all goes so quickly.' One day, he was walking in the street in the city when he looked up and saw his dead father, grey hair, greying moustache, the look in his eyes. It was himself, his own reflection that he saw in the shop window.

He taught us how to measure the Southern Cross in the night sky, how to find our way south.

*

The chest pain was his, not mine; I was just the one who felt it, as probably he did himself. Like me, he had told no one. Like me, he wanted nothing to get in the way of my visit. But he had seen me, had heard his granddaughter playing the violin, and then he died. The way he left was in keeping with his life and his character: he was out there, on his own, ahead of anyone, solitary, exact and precise. At the shopping centre he fell once, then stood up and said he wanted to go home. He said he was fine, and walked, and then he fell again. The ambulance took an inordinately long time to come, and there were people who helped, who saw to him in his last moments. My niece Eden said, 'Grandpa's heart is in my heart. My heart is in his heart.' Our younger daughter, Rebecca, said, 'It was quick, like diving into a pool of water quickly.' Eden said, 'Did you come to South Africa because Grandpa died?' She had the chronology wrong, but I thought to myself, yes, that is the reason I came.

The memorial lecture for Bram Fischer went ahead in Cape Town without me. If I did not make it to the Houses of Parliament, my father did, because he was mentioned there as my absence was explained. Strangely, one of my purposes in writing the book had lain in a certain feeling for Fischer's daughters, Ruth and Ilse, who themselves had been through so much, not least the painful deaths of their mother and father and their brother. There was another unusual connection, because early on, talking to the two sisters at Ruth's house in Melville in Johannesburg, I discovered that I had the same birthday as Bram Fischer. Ilse called it, with the Afrikaans pronunciation, *spokery*—magic, ghosting, uncanny—and had said, 'Now you have to write the book.' Now again she called it a kind of 'spooking'. As my book was bringing Ruth and Ilse's father back to life, my own father had died. Writing had crisscrossed with life and seemed to cancel it out. Lorraine, who had been the one to encourage me to study overseas on the day the Soweto Uprising of 1976 began—Ilse's birthday, as it happened, though I did not know it at the time—remarked to Ilse, 'Stephen's life has these patterns.'

✳

It seemed to me that when I had seen him on the Sunday and early Monday, along with the temper and impetuosity, there was a beauty, an inner clarity my father had developed in older age. Now, in the Jewish way, the funeral was held quickly. My uncle Stanley flew in from London, my uncle Michael was there—my father's brothers, to see him to rest. At the cemetery, my brother and I had our shirts ripped in the ceremonial custom. We went in to see and identify my father, and my mother came as well. I touched his face and felt how cold he was. The men who had helped him said he had looked peaceful, but now his eyes were blackened, his own birthmarks, and there was sand from Jerusalem on his face. Why would they do that, my mother said, feeling the earth already on him. This was holy ground, but holy ground is what you make of it, and he would be buried in South Africa.

Shakespeare's bare lines came: 'Poor Tom's a-cold'; 'Put out the light, and then put out the light'. Yet when we buried him in the red soil in Johannesburg, still wet from the rain, I looked around and saw how beautiful it was. Here was the *koppie*, the rocky outcrop of hill under the sky, with its inimitable African clouds, with its scarcely credible beauty. There were the trees, there were the rocks, there the city, there the birds, there the grasses, here the stones, here the earth. To stay here forever, looking out, becoming part of this earth, is a prospect worth contemplating: by no means the worst place to be. He had been as wild, infuriating, lovable as ever, and that was how he would stay.

I wrote out these notes between three and four o'clock on the night of my father's funeral. 'Go well, stay well, go in peace, remain in peace.' Our lives are changed forever. We must find a new way to live now. But the past must be part of it too, at its heart, beating and alive.

In the Air

⤢ 55

It is late September or early October 1977 in the early hours of the morning, and I am somewhere off the west coast of Africa flying towards England to begin my life there as a student. I have new boots on my feet, a fresh haircut, a notebook, a window next to me on my right, the dark outside. It has been a tumultuous time. Beginning just over a year ago, the country has been in turmoil as resistance has swirled from town to town, community to community, school to school. The repression has also been worse than ever: organisations banned, leaders on the run, young black men and women heading out of the country in their thousands to join the ANC in Tanzania and elsewhere. Detention without trial has become the natural order, and there are regular deaths in prison, explained only in the most surreal forms as people somehow slip on bars of soap or fall from open windows. People have been killed in the hundreds, there have been mass arrests, a generation is being schooled for the fierce disciplines of revolution. We at our mostly white university have held our protests, some have been arrested, we have learned our marginality, have tried to find ways of living up to our responsibilities. And yet a feeling of gloom prevails, almost tangible as the atmosphere we live in: what will show us a way out of this? I have stood in our house with my mother, the lights off, as we heard feet running alongside our walls and through the garden.

As the plane hurtles on its way through the night, this is not flight or escape as such, more like a tether being lengthened. And yet there

246

is also the feeling that I am like a seed being launched on the wind, set to land in foreign parts, perhaps to take root there, perhaps to set up a base for others to come. The weight of the night is on me, and yet there are also lights if I look out of the window, beacons of their own kind. Some of them are above: they are stars. Some of them are below: they are ships, lights on the sea. If I imagine carefully, I can picture the plane upside down. It could be upside down, so that the lights above are the ships, the lights below are the stars, and I let myself feel this for a while. We are flying above the still earth, but the earth too is in movement, spinning on its axis and swinging in its orbit, the sun and planets circling the galaxy, the galaxy spinning and moving who knows where into the deepest depths. The night outside is like the sea, the sea is like space, and only the lights above and below seem to mark their mysterious way. This is my birthmark, where I have been, where I am going. Right side up, upside down, in a place where motion is everything and nothing, here I am in a capsule of time and space gazing out at the dense and sparkling night, and who knows where I am headed or what I will find.

☞ Afterword

This is a story refracted through the prism of my recollections. It began its life for two main reasons. First, I had the memories in my mind, and did not want them simply to disappear through the generations, as happens especially when migration is involved. Second, the impulse is that of the case study, with my own life as its focus. The account, in other words, is an attempt to understand how one existence took on a particular trajectory. In this my approach was primarily one of interested curiosity: how things came to be this way. And to wonder at the extraordinary spectrum of experience and texture any life has, how we all have our 'birthmarks'.

For that reason, among others, nothing in this story was written out of anger or rancour, just the quest to understand the terms and circumstances of a particular character who happens in this instance to be both subject and object. I also know that others will remember these events differently, have their own stories to tell.

I am grateful to numbers of people without whose support writing this account would not have been possible, and also to those who read and responded to earlier versions. I am especially indebted to family and friends who tolerated these excursions into memory. My brief account of the relationship to the Lithuanian past that lay behind my grandparents' experience is inevitably inflected by Dan Jacobson's remarkable book *Heshel's Kingdom* (and W.G. Sebald's reference to it in *Austerlitz*). I am particularly appreciative of a fellowship at the Stellenbosch Institute for Advanced Study, where the book came within sight of becoming whole.